Practical Telepathy

(1924)

Joseph Ovette

ISBN 0-7661-0634-9

OTHER BOOKS BY THE SAME AUTHOR

"MAGICIAN'S NEW FIELD"
(1918)

"TRICKERY TRICKS"
(1918)

"ADVANCE MAGIC"
(1919)

"GRANDDADDY'S OLD ARMCHAIR"
or
"THE TRIPLE MYSTERY"
(1919)

"VAUDEVILLE MAGIC"
(In Collaboration with David J. Lustig)
(1919)

"BARGAIN MAGIC"
(1920)

* * *

In Preparation
"NEW ERA MAGIC"

PRACTICAL TELEPATHY

A Technical Treatise in Non-Tecnical Language
Designed to Benefit the Profesional and Amateur, and to Give a Broader Insight Into
One of the Most Fascinating
Branches of Public
Entertaining.

By JOSEPH OVETTE

Revised, Edited and Illustrated
By PRESTON LANGLEY HICKEY

THE REILLY COMPANY
Publishers
Chicago, Illinois
1924

Copyright 1924
THE REILLY COMPANY
Chicago

EDITOR'S INTRODUCTION

After enriching the literary field of the magical fraternity with six works dealing strictly with sleight-of-hand, general tricks and illusions, within the past five years, namely, MAGICIAN'S NEW FIELD, 1918; TRICKERY TRICKS, 1918; ADVANCED MAGIC, 1919; GRANDDADDY'S OLD ARMCHAIR, *or* THE TRIPLE MYSTERY, *in manuscript form, 1919;* VAUDEVILLE MAGIC, *in collaboration with David J. Lustig, 1919, and* BARGAIN MAGIC, *1920, Joseph Ovette, renowned exponent of necromancy and writer along the lines of the allied arts has, at last, penned the present volume,* PRACTICAL TELEPATHY.

From out of the yesterdays of the author's many years of practical experience in appearing before the American theatre-going public and those of other countries; in which he has been through practically every phase of the stage, from private entertainments to the carnival sideshow; carnival to vaudeville and then to the road show of his own, in which he specialized in Chinese magic, he has drawn upon his vast knowledge and given to the world a book rich in the fruits of a life study.

It has been both a pleasure and an education to this writer to have been chosen from out of the many who, perhaps, were more capable of handling the task, to revise and edit this work for presentation to the fraternity.

If the vast number of books on Telepathy and Mind Reading now in existence, were the determining factor as to whether or not there were already enough books treating this subject, there would certainly be no excuse for the appearance of this volume, but numbers do not, necessarily, always supply the need.

Books on Telepathy and Mind Reading, as far as most of those which have come to our notice go, have been very vague and reticent regarding the practical working of the art. Only failure would confront the at-

tempt to work the game if only information gleaned from such books as have heretofore appeared, were depended upon.

The purpose of this volume is three-fold. In the words of the author himself:

"First: To furnish the said 'peculiar' and 'select knowledge' in the form of remarkably clever secrets including those which have been locked within the silent memory of the very sparsely few, for past decades; some of which cost the writer of this book 'blood-money' for single features alone.

"Second: We have been preparing many years for this exposure. The time is now at hand, and we lay everything bare without reserve. Our purpose is to disseminate this knowledge so that it may have a wider range of usefulness, regardless of the turmoil which the expose may provoke from among the few.

"Third: The exposition of secrets which have never been sold nor advertised, nor even whispered about, because, for one reason, they are new; the very latest twists and the last word in the art of creating baffling Psychic Effects. It should always be remembered that the extent of profit or pleasure which the ownership of this book may afford, depends largely on the reader's ability to guard its secrets."

The above statements are, in themselves, self-explanatory as to the purpose of this book. Nothing more need be said, except, perhaps, a repetition of what has been written before, the hope that the reader may derive as much pleasure and knowledge from the reading as the editor did from the task which is now ended.

                PRESTON LANGLEY HICKEY.

EMERY LYLE,
Chicago, Ill.
August, 1924.

CHAPTER ONE

PRACTICAL TELEPATHY

CHAPTER ONE

GENERAL INTRODUCTORY AND SEALED LETTER INTERPOLATIONS.

(Being merely a foretaste and miniature exposition of what this volume holds in store for its owner; showing, not only the possibilities of clever manipulation in the field of PSYCHIC PHENOMENA but samples of ASTOUNDING EFFECTS which ARE BEING CREATED—not where mere gall is depended upon, but where the GUIDING PRINCIPLE IS *SCIENCE!*)

Garbed in Hindu costume, we will say, (for effect) the performer appears and addresses his audience somewhat as follows:

"Ladies and gentlemen: We wish it clearly understood that we make no claim to the supernatural; our demonstrations are offered simply as form of entertainment, leaving to you individually, to apply your own construction and judgment to the problems.

"Should we succeed in our endeavor to afford you with interesting thinking material, we shall feel that our object has been well served.

"I propose this afternoon, to answer questions for any persons in the audience. My assistant will now pass among you and distribute slips of paper on which to write your questions. After writing your questions, sign your name, fold the slip, place it in the enevlope and SEAL." (Assistant leaves stage and passes out the slips and envelopes to the audience.)

(No attempt is made to furnish slips to all, but only to those who signify a desire to write questions. Demonstrator can regulate very easily the number of questions for the time he has allotted to this part of his program, without encroaching or crowding out other features he may have on his list, by simply limiting the number of slips and envelopes to be distributed.)

As soon as all slips are given out, assistants immediately pass up and down the aisle again, carrying canes, at the ends of which are attached GLASS GLOBES (ordinary fish prisons,) which are reached out in front of each of the rows of spectators, enabling those who wish to deposit in the globes, their sealed questions.

After envelopes are all collected, the assistants take globes upon the stage and place them in a row upon a long narrow table, detaching the canes which they take with them behind the scenes.

The sealed envelopes have not for one moment, left the sight of the audience. His psychicinsky strides forth, and, taking a standing position behind the table, incidentally showing—apparently without purpose, that his hands are clean, draws up his sleeves slightly, and solemnly, but ostentatiously dips thumb and finger into first bowl bringing forth one of the envelopes. Holding the envelope up so all can see it, he looks at it intently for an instant only, CALLS OUT THE NAME AND READS OFF THE QUESTION *BEFORE OPENING ENVELOPE,* and begins at once to answer the question while he proceeds to cut the envelope open, when he finds he made a slight mistake, as he discovers the initials are D. W. instead of W. D.

Now, while making perhaps, more of an apology than is really necessary in the circumstances, he dips in a bowl again and brings forth another envelope, which he reads as before, or in similar manner, and ALWAYS BEFORE OPENING THE ENVELOPE!

So, on he proceeds to read all the sealed names and questions until all are thus disposed of and *answered.*

POINTS OF FACT: Sealed envelopes never leave sight of the audience. No side-tracking or switching. No apparatus used. No chemicals or alcohol. Globes are the ordinary fish variety—made for fish habitation, and UN-

PRACTICAL TELEPATHY

PREPARED. Performer ACTUALLY reads all the questions collected, and IN FULL VIEW!

EXPLANATION: The reading of the first question is only a pretense. The performer merely calls out a name—ANY NAME and quotes, or recites a question of HIS OWN MAKE-UP! Now, as he proceeds to answer this question—which is a fake—he opens the envelope and finds the question CORRECT, also the name was correctly defined — except getting the initials REVERSED—which is quite unimportant. Now he takes up another (a second envelope), and pretends, as before, to read the name and question enclosed therein. What he does, is to call out the name and question WHICH HE FOUND ON OPENING THE FIRST ENVELOPE!

Now, while answering this question, he proceeds to open the second envelope, and finds the name and question correct (?) At least, SO HE SAYS. Now when he holds up the THIRD ENVELOPE and pretends to read its contents; what he does is to call out the name and question which the SECOND ENVELOPE ENCLOSED! Thus he proceeds until all questions are answered—ALWAYS CALLING OUT THE NAME AND QUESTION WHICH HE FOUND ENCLOSED IN THE ENVELOPE IMMEDIATELY PRECEDING! This is, no doubt, the best, as well as the simplest method EVER DEVISED!

It is well, however, to have more than one method so as not to be obliged to use any one at two performances in success. This not only shows versatility and resourcefulness, but throws the foxy ones OFF THE SCENT, so to speak.

EFFECT NUMBER TWO

This experiment is, in plain English a COLD KNOCK-OUT—a CRUSHING BAFFLER! The envelopes are collected in a square box by the assistant who then places the recepticle in which are the questions

PRACTICAL TELEPATHY

on the performer's table *in full view of the audience.* There is no exchange of boxes—the envelopes are NOT carried back stage and the container in which the questions are COLLECTED, remains in FULL VIEW ALL THE TIME, before and during the reading.

Also, the performer DOES NOT OPEN THE ENVELOPES *AT ALL,* but reads them WHILE THEY ARE SEALED! He holds the envelopes in his hands while reading their contents, and as soon as he has finished answering each question, he writes name and question on the outside of the envelope; then grasps the corner of the sealed envelope between the first and second fingers, and giving it a vigorous flip, sends it spinning through the air to the party who answers to the name which it bears, so that the party can break the seal himslef and

PLATE ONE

PRACTICAL TELEPATHY

IDENTIFY HIS OWN WRITING AND QUESTION AS CORRECT!

The reading takes place in full view, while facing the audience. NO ALCOHOL NOR APPARATUS IS USED!

EXPLANATION: The box can be square or cylindrical in shape, but it is *double*. It is one box loosely nestled within another. The inner box has a bottom and is held within the outer one by means of a little catch. The outside box or shell, carries a quarter inch flange which conceals the inner box at the mouth. A bale is attached to the outer box or shell for carrying purposes, and to hang on the end of a cane or pole so as to enable the assistant to reach in between the aisles where the latter are too far apart for all conveniences.

Now the table on which the box is deposited, has a lower shelf (see sketch). The drapery should extend to just below the shelf—but clear the floor by six or eight inches.

This drapery should be rich and gaudy and bear a fancy design and lettering in gold. For exceptional adornment, a brocaded portrait of the artist might also be added.

The table top has a tray over which box of questions is placed. The assistant sitting on the shelf, back to audience; with pen-knife or scissors in one hand and pencil close by, opens the trap in the table top and allows the inner box with its contents to slide into his possession. The assistant now gets busy at once—opens the envelopes—writes questions on the outside of NEW ENVELOPES—encloses original slips and seals. As soon as gets a half dozen or so of the questions ready, he places them on the BOTTOM of the box which he has REVERSED, and slips the inverted box through the trap and into the shell. This enables the performer to begin reading the questions without delay. He takes out one envelope at a time and he reads them. After he has read a dozen or so, it becomes only natural to dip the

PRACTICAL TELEPATHY

hand DEEPER into the box where he can take them direct from the assistant's hand while they are nice and fresh. Or, better still, the assistant can place the questions on a little ledge provided within the shell, and the performer can help himself as he gets ready for them.

EFFECT NUMBER THREE

At the third performance of your engagement, should it be a prolonged one, you can use the first method described, or, if you prefer, you can work the experiment by the method to be outlined herewith.

The assistants collect the folded slips—(questions)—in cylinder shaped box; the description of which is depicted in the accompanying sketch.

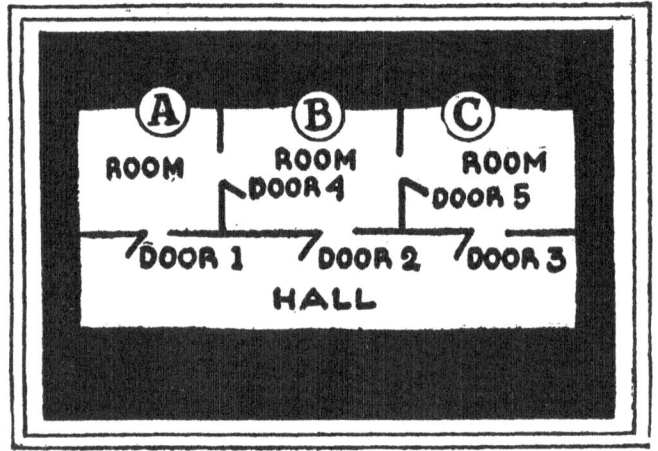

PLATE TWO

There is a partition in the center. The lower space contains "Yesterday's slips" or blanks. The lids which cover each end are EXACTLY ALIKE. In collecting the puestions; the lid for the end in which the puestions are deposited, is off—of course—and hanging by a thread at the side of the box.

PRACTICAL TELEPATHY

When the slips are collected, the lid is put on and the box carried by its handle, is taken upon the stage; on the way thereto, the assistant turns it over, i. e., OTHER END UP. This is done merely by turning the handle in the hand. He can whirl the box over several times, in full view, if he feels sporty, but he must know which end is up or down. He can distinguish this by secretly marking the handle.

Approaching the table, the assistant removes the top cover and, tipping the box over, dumps slips (yesterday'ss) in a pile on the table and walks off (unconcernedly), behind the scenes, with the GENUINE SLIPS! Well out of view, the assistant dumps the questions out of the box and proceeds to read them and then write the names of the questioners and the questions on the outside of the respective slips.

When this is accomplished the assistant puts them in a large crystal bowl which is prepared as follows:

The bowl is none other than the kind used as a habitation for captive fish. A partion dividing the interior into two compartments is made by cutting sheet celluloid to fit the inside of the bowl; both sides of the improvised partition being smoothly covered with tin-foil. After the partition is finished, it is rolled up and inserted through the mouth of the bowl and glued in place all around to hold it firm in the center of the bowl.

There is also a foot-piece on which the bowl rests. The assistant brings out the bowl—places it on the table and gathers up the pile of slips and puts them in the bowl, in front—(empty compartment)—and forgets (?) to place it on its pedestal.

About the time the questions are being collected from the audience the performer gets into the midst of a very interesting experiment. This gives the assistant the necessary time to do his part. Soon after the bowl has been brought out, however, the performer finishes his absorbing demonstration or lecture, and turns his attention to the next thing on the program, which is the reading of the questions.

PRACTICAL TELEPATHY

The performer picks up bowl—holds it up as if to call attention to it and as he transfers it to the left hand, the bowl naturally gets a half-turn. This brings the compartment holding the genuine slips to the front, in which position performer places bowl on the foot. The reading of the puestions can continue until all are answered.

It will be noted that the movements in this method, too, are all *perfectly natural,* and coherently successive,— therefore PERFECT IN EFFECT, and indetectable to anyone except perhaps, some of the "knowing ones" who may be able to reason it out.

There is practically no danger of making a failure of it. The questions can, of course, be sealed, and for best effect, should be.

EFFECT NUMBER FOUR

There are a class of performers who take great delight in doing things in the most difficult or complexed way. The more elaborate and complicated the apparatus—the more does it apparently meet with their fancy. For the benefit of this class of aspirants, I suggest the following:

Go to a dealer in electrical supplies and procure a dictagraph and ear connections (multi-acoustocon). Get an electrician, one who knows his business, to rig it up for you, so you can get spoken words direct from dressing room to stage. Have your "Mat" behind a table.— (straw matting is best suited). We advise against working this system among audience, as it is out of date and too well known, owing to frequent exposure, for perfect safety. However, it might do on stage O. K.

Copper plates are attached to soles of shoes and wire passes up thru pants leg, under upper garments to back of head. Ear piece is attached to whalebone covered with cloth and fitted over head holding ear-piece in place as used by telephone operators. Turban on head is arranged to *conceal all.*

Wire connects dictograph with center of mat. Now by standing on mat all rigged up for business when your

PRACTICAL TELEPATHY

assistant talks in dictograph, you can hear what he says as plainly as by telephone message. This enables the performer to read the FAKE questions, as tho they were GENUINE by gazing into a crystal ball or by the use of any other fake he may choose for effect. But after all of this bother and expense—clumsy, and cumbersome arrangement, you gain nothing, and, if anything the effect you produce is less perfect and mystifying than are the effects produced by the three simple methods which we have hereinbefore described.

CHAPTER TWO

PRACTICAL TELEPATHY

CHAPTER TWO

POINTERS ON QUALIFICATIONS, NATURAL AND OTHERWISE, ESSENTIAL TO SUCCESSFUL EXPLOITATION OF MIND READING—DEALING WITH ANSWERS IN SOMNOLENCY INCLUDING "STOCK QUESTIONS," "BOOSTERS" AND ANSWERS TO MISCELLANEOUS AND GENERAL QUESTIONS.

The aspirant to a MIND-READING CAREER for either vaudeville or clubs, should first make sure that he or she has talent for an act of that nature. A mind-reader, to be successful, should and must be full of life, energy and imagination, be magnetic and have the faculty to think at a flash. Well posted, especially in the topics of the day, he or she should also have a sense of humor.

Telepathy is rich in the opportunity for comedy. However, be absolutely sure that what you "pull" for humor, is HUMOROUS. Never try to make a fool of a spectator, and your answers should always be civil and respectful unless "some simp gets fresh and tries to crab the works." Even then you should not become vindictive, but merely turn the incident into a humorous channel at his expense. Comedy is SPICE for entertainment, but it should not be ALL SPICE, or you may detract seriously from the mystery of your efforts which, in the long run, are the main thing.

HOW SOME "MIND READERS" ANSWER QUESTIONS

To give the reader an idea how questions are handled by some "mind-Readers"—I offer the following examples:

"You will find the lost ring, which you missed ten days ago, in your ink-well! You will remember the ink was spilled: Well, a child did that; she was playing with the ring and DROPPED IT INTO THE BOTTLE. Trying to regain the ring she SPILLED THE INK." (2) "You had unexpected company just as you were taking a bath. You will find the ring in the BATHROOM." (3) "You were cleaning your jewelry—you removed the ring to clean it at the same time. The ring got brushed off onto the floor and *rolled under sofa*. You did not miss it for 36 hours. IT IS THERE YET! When you go home, look where I've told you, and if you don't find ring, come here and I'll forfeit $100.00 thru the management of this theatre." (Good bluff for opening night!)

FAKE NAMES

Performer calls out faked name—of course no one raises hand. Performer remarks, "I don't blame you—that's not your name. You came here thinking you could fool me. You want to know if your wife is true to you. If you were as true to your wife as she is to you, you wouldn't ask me such a question. If it wasn't for your wife, I would tell your name here!"

ANOTHER FAKE NAMEs You want to know if Jeff will ever be as tall as Mut."

Answer: "No, but Mut would be as SMALL as Jeff some day if he did some of the things you are doing!"

Question: "Why was the ocean built so near the shore?"

Answer: (1) "So that the waves can KISS THE BEACH and CARESS THE PRETTY BATHERS. (2) To prevent bathers from getting too fresh, (salt water). (3) To cool the fever of love and wash away the stains of soiled human conscience, as well as to temporarily reduce the size of feet!"

Question: "Will I ever marry?"

Answer: "Of course you will—that's the big hope of life!"

Question: "When will I marry?"

Answer: (If male) "Just as soon as you can convince some lady that she wants you."

Question: "I lost a sum of money—where can I find it?"

Answer: "Not lost—but stolen, no recovery."

Question: "I have not heard from my aunt for ten years."

Answer: "Re-write your question—mail it, or leave it at the Box Office, and I will give you an answer within 48 hours."

Question: "Give me the name of the person who stole my watch."

Answer: "I cannot give such information in public."

Question: "Would I be better off if I left (naming town)?"

Answer: "No, but (naming town) would be better off if you left."

Question: "Will I marry the girl I am going with now?"

Answer: "You are closer to her than I am—ask her."

Question: "What are my lucky days?"

Answer: "Get a horoscope. It's free." (Performer should have horoscopes of each month printed for gratis distribution to those wishing to know what's best suited to them or their children, etc.)

Question: "Would I be more successful in another business?"

Answer: "I do not advise an immediate change, for your success comes only through hard work, faith in your own ability, honesty with yourself and your fellow men."

Question: "Did George Washington ever tell a lie?"

Answer: "When I die and go to heaven, I'll ask him

ofr you, and if he is not there then you may ask him for me."

You have, perhaps, met and corresponded, at some time, with persons of whom you have sought information and who perhaps answered your questions correctly without betraying their own secrets or business. This is a study in itself; it is not necessary that the lady or man should be highly educated—all that is required is that she or he should be a good talker, not nervous, and must be able to read any kind of writing at a glance. The lady or man should make a study of the STOCK REPLIES. A good way is to memorize them, so as to always have a suitable answer ready, even if she or he does not answer them word for word. But the safest way is to consult this list, and after you get possession of the questions, and after they are developed, copy each question on separate paper, first copying the writer's name. (Some performers request their audiences to sign their initials only—it is more effective when a person is first called by their full name by the Mind-Reader,—then the question. Then select a suitable answer from the list and write it below the question, each on separate slips—small square block paper will do—these are placed one on top of the other and concealed in dress (bosom).

If you decide to use one or two "boosters" perhaps three, the Mind-Reader has the booster questions and replies memorized. These are called *"Stock Questions,"* and should always border on the sensation. As an example, I will give you an idea. For instance you call a fake name who writes: "I lost my pocket book, can you locate it?"

Answer: "You are always blaming other people for your own carelessness. Your pocket-book is not lost; it is wedged between the second drawer and back wall of your dresser. When you get home—look and you will find it there."

Supposing you have a lady "booster" among the audience—at Ladies' Matinee (no men admitted): She writes the following *Stock Message*:

1. Do you know my condition?
2. Can you locate him?

SENSATIONAL ANSWERS

1. Yes I know your condition—you are about to become a mother.
2. Your lover is at Pasadena, Califorina. He has not deserted you. You will hear from him soon. He will marry you.

This makes all the ladies talk. I used a female disguised—one from my own company. No one knew her. No name should be signed to stock questions—use initials. I never use boosters only when I want to work something sensational so as to increase business. In small time places don't use them But when a performer plays opera houses with his own show, he has to work up business on one week stands. Of course, it is up to the professor's showmanship to produce novel billings, newspaper dope and sensational sruff for the 'Stock" biz. The lady should always read the stock messages first, without cloth or blindfold; and then after she gets thru with these she is blindfolded or large cloth thrown over her. If the latter, the right hand should be left on outside of cloth to gesticulate with, and the other hand is used to handle the slips of paper—questions and replies.

Of course, for the TELEPHONE SYSTEM, the third party—the operator, has to communicate all of this.

THE ANSWERS

Always read your stock questions and answers first—boosters, if you intend to use them. You have to use them if you want to work sensational stuff—something that will make the ladies talk.

1. I see! I see! I see! I have thought of a lady sitting to my left—her name is Mrs. Mitler. She is

PRACTICAL TELEPATHY

worried, worried, worried; she wants to know if her father is to have an operation.

"No, my dear, he will not undergo an operation. He will be well enough without it, to love and be with you."

2. Yes, yes, yes, Mrs. Jones, your home will be happier for the element that has entered it. Any unhappiness will surely disappear. This coming change regarding that party, will set all differences at rest, and you will be happy and the SUN WILL SHINE!

3. Mrs. McDonald, who is present in the fourth row, left, wants to know if hubby is true to her.

Yes, yes, you are fortunate enough to have that sort of husband. You are indeed fortunate.

Frivolous—
    4. You must learn to be sensible.

Brooding—
    5. You must not allow your mind to dwell on any one thing too much.

Reason to be Grateful—
    6. You have a pleasing appearance.

Short on Self-Reliance—
    7. You have not sufficient self-esteem.

Absent Minded—
    8. You lose and misplace many things.

True Blue—
    9. You are loyal to your friends.

Too Inquisitive—
    10. You have a habit of asking too many questions.

The shorter replies are called SWITCHING a question around using short replies to the first. Lady has answered them all right without giving much information. I do this only on foolish and difficult or perhaps lengthy questions. Always give good replies to earnest questions. When you get more familiar as to the finer points of somnolency you can then distinguish the good questions at a glance when developing them in operating room. It is not necessary to answer all questions—pick out the good ones—ten to fifteen for small time—20 to 25 for big time, and the stock questions to open with, and the predictions to close with. It fills out the time.

11. Ah! Miss Dunsberry: I can tell you—you know I can, that you will be married in two years, as the answer to your question must be. You go out occasionally with a certain gentleman—BUT HE IS NOT THE ONE. Oh, dear, no! The one you will marry will come to you sometime during the coming year, and he will bring you more love than you have ever dreamed of. It will be real, real, *real!*

12. Mrs. Johnson, I can answer your questions very quickly. As to a child—one will come to you. Mark my words, and remember what I say—This child will be talented. (Use this for ladies matinees).

Sees Only the Dark Side of Things—

13. You are forever looking for trouble.

Too Noisy—

14. You worry and fret over things that do not concern you.

Extravagance—

15. You try to live beyond your means, that's why you are poor.

Err in Confidence—

16. You have too much faith in human nature.

Clinging Vine—

17. You are too affectionate.

Beneficient—

18. You have a great desire to help others.

Nature's Divinest Instinct—

19. You are a natural lover.

Magnanamous—

20. You are noble, generous and good.

Qualities That Make for Success—

21. Imagination and perseverance hold the key to riches for you.

Hide Not Good Qualities Under a Bushel—

22. You must cultivate an opinion of yourself. You do your work well, so do not be afraid to let people know it.

Too Pussy-foot—

23. You say you were born in March? You will accomplish little until you have first gained the courage to "SPEAK OUT" and defend your convictions.

Need of Courage—

24. You harbor the thought that you may not be able to make a financial success. If you think that way—you may not be able to do it.

Timid and Short on Business Sagacity—

25. Have confidence—plenty of it—in your personal powers. Keep close tab on the person with whom you are dealing.

Deficient in Will Power—

26. Will it in your mind that you will do a certain thing—repeat the proposition six or seven times—THEN DO IT—YOU CAN DO IT IF YOU TRY.

Constructive Genius—

27. You are not an originator, but you can take an idea and work it out in detail. You can make practical ideas into things that would remain merely dreams with the inventor.

Perseverence—

28. Much comes of your success in your ability to rebound from defeat or disaster.

Determination Needed—

29. Stop worrying and fussing and make yourself calm—*you can do it*. Your success depends not only on what you want, but on how MUCH you want it.

Tactless—

30. Stop criticizing—try suggesting and use this energy toward winning in your economic struggle.

Trusting to Luck—

31. Don't be in a hurry and start without any plan—concentration, will, in time give you a well defined plan of action, and this you must have to gain success.

Wisdom Wanted—

32. The wise man investigates before he condemns, but the fool condemns blindly.

Procrastination—

33. Make it something which will help you TOWARD perfect success and wealth. Perhaps it will be only one step—the next step may be easier, and you will be stronger. Begin NOW—learn TODAY to do it. Yesterday never returns. "Tomorrow never comes." Today means NOW!

PRACTICAL TELEPATHY

Slumbering Giant—

34. You are naturally possessed with strong personal magnetism. Apply it to your every day life—to customers, employer or friends. If you make proper use of this gift it will make your life's path smoother and bring you PRESTIGE, POWER AND WEALTH.

Straight Ahead—

35. You are on the ROAD TO SUCCESS—keep in the middle of it—Don't make a change of business.

Investments—

36. Real estate investments will bring you wealth.

Best Thing to Do—

37. You had better sell that invention of yours. There will be more money in it for you if you sell it outright.

Uneasy—

38. You will receive a letter from the party soon that will give you the desired information.

Every Little Bit Helps—

39. There is a small inheritance coming to you from a relative whom you have never met.

Not Advisable to Switch—

40. You had better stick to the fellow whom you have in mind. He is all right. If you make the change you'll be sorry.

Friday O. K.—

41. You say you were born in May—Friday the 13th is your lucky day.

April Fools (?)—

42. You say you were born in April? People born

in this month are never satisfied and are very changeable.

Charity Begins at Home—

43. You spend your time and energy worrying over other people's troubles; they are not worrying over yours! You lose golden opportunities by wasting time thru this.

The Merry Month of June—

44. You say you were born in June—People born in this month know EXACTLY what they want and are never satisfied with anything less than full justice, and they always rely on their brains and common sense to attain it.

Human Reason is Nature's Masterpiece—

45. Be guided by your own reason—watch your surroundings carefully as you are easily influenced by this.

Business is Gambling—

46. Don't invest your money in that deal. If you do you, will lose it all—take my advice.

Don't Insist on Being Born in July—

47. You say you were born in July. People born in this month never know what they want. Generally very nervous. They can make a bushel of trouble out of nothing and then have nothing left to make others worry. Your lucky day is Friday 13th.

Wake Up!—

48. Don't waste your life in dreams—nothing in it.

Put the Harness on Your Ability—

49. You have knowledge, turn it to account. Go into business for yourself.

A Cold Month With a Warm Heart—
  50. People born in January are good natured. The only way you can get into trouble is in trying to do things for others. Most days are your lucky days.

Imagination Needs Anchoring—
  51. You imagine things. The lightest thing on earth is imagination. Forget it!

Lucky Dog—
  52. A man is coming to you to make you a mighty fine offer. It means success for you. Accept it. He appreciates your talents.

Do Rich Relations Ever Die?
  53. To gain riches you must not wait for some relative to die. You must act. Do it today. You are a hustler and attend to business.

Born With Harness On—
  54. People born in February make the best farmers. Wednesday is their lucky day.

Not a Clairvoyant—
  55. You cannot tell what it is until you try it.

Waiting for Something to Turn Up—
  56. You are thinking of some force or power to gain what you are after. You must cultivate fearlessness.

Act on the Psychological—
  57. You lack will power. Sometimes you are in a magnetic state of mind. This is the time to seek what you want.

Anger—
  58. Your temper comes in an outburst; it has lost you friends and money. Try and control yourself. You can do it if you try.

You Should Worry(?)—
   59. You are to inherit a lot of money, so you will be wealthy some day.

Bravery—
   60. Those who are born in August are strong minded. They know not what fear is; they are not afraid to invest money in any business. Tuesday is their most successful day.

Trustworthy—
   61. Do not doubt the person you mention. Accept the offer. It means success for you.

Innocent of the Capers of Fate—
   62. Do not make that trip, it means disaster.

Has a Pull with Destiny—
   63. Your luck comes unexpected always. You will never be rich but you will never want for anything. A happy old age is in store for you.

On the Right Track—
   64. You are planning to build a house for two. Go to it. It will bring you rest, and while you are resting, it will improve and double in value in five years time. You are lucky.

Time is as Limitless as Space—
   65. You try to do too many things at one time. Do one thing at a time. There is time for everything, yet there is no time like the present.

Reckless with Push—
   66. Yes, of course, you know who you are, but do you know what you are? You try to get to the top of the ladder too quickly. You will fail if you don't put on the brakes.

Solitude for Preference—
   67. Those who are born in September are slow in

seeing things; they like to be alone. Sunday is their lucky day.

Not so Bad After All—
68. Your money which you lost by an unforseen occurrence, will be returned to you. Don't worry over it.

Ignorant of Own Talents—
69. You can double your earning power if you will use your talents in the right way. Have patience, it will make you prosperous and happy.

A Lawsuit is a Cobweb of Steal—
70. That money matter you speak of will not bring you success. It will involve a lawsuit and perhaps you know what that means.

Capacity Needs Room to Expand—
71. People born in October are ambitious; big cities are the best place for them to do business in. Mondays are their lucky days.

Method—
72. It's not always just what you do, but the method you employ to gain your ends, which generally counts most. If you do it right you will win that party over all right. It means something to do this.

Backward—
73. Cultivate will power, it will make you master of your own fate.

Easy Mark, Maybe—
74. Some people take advantage of your good nature—be more serious.

Tears and Iimber Lip—
75. You are drifting—Don't waste your energy on needless fretting and whining. The big prizes

go to those who produce something that the world needs.

Lack of Care in Selecting Help—
76. Better look for friends who can boost you over the top—not for those who can merely entertain you. The latter brings you nothing.

Study Your Associates—
77. If you would become successful and rich, associate with those who are successful, or who are ambitious to get on.

Loose Thinking—
78. Born in November? I'm afraid you are a busybody and in business matters generally, you have too many irons in the fire. Learn to CONCENTRATE. Thursday is your luckiest day.

Self-reliance Needed—
79. Don't depend on that party, the experience gained in fighting your own battles, will help you to win out in most things you attempt. Don't depend on others, if you do you might lose out.

Action vs. Talk—
80. The best way for you to get ahead is to plan carefully, but don't talk about what you are going to do—do it!

Faith—
81. The party you are enquiring about will return unexpectedly. Keep faith, it is for your own good.

Possibilities of Personal Magnetism—
82. Develop your will power and magnetism, and you will achieve any object you set your mind on.

Throw Bouquets at Yourself—

83. You are your own enemy; you hate yourself. You should think that you are happy. You are well and prosperous. Think that you are a human magnet; think that you are lucky and that desirable things come to you naturally.

Refuse to be Born in December—

84. People born in December have no confidence in themselves or in anyone else. They are naturally born faultfinders. They criticize everybody but themselves. They are conceited. They have no lucky day.

Pedestrianism as a Blessing—

85. Trouble, fear, worry and bad temper are your weakness. You can overcome these by taking long walks by yourself.

Care in Choosing Friends—

86. Don't trust that friend too much; you might regret it. Stick to your old friends.

As to Business—

87. You have fine perceptive powers and will succeed in the business you mention. You are a natural leader—push it along; there is money in it for you.

Wasting Time—

88. You are wasting your time on the party you mention. Be careful.

Too Confiding—

89. You have given that party too much information already; that is your weakness. You trust other people too much.

Fickle Minded—

90. You say you were born in January; you must

conquer your fickle, changeable nature. Make definite plans, then nothing in the world can hold you back. Friday is your lucky day.

Blessed Human Sunshine—
91. You are the maker of your own destiny. You are naturally cheerful, bright, jolly and happy. Sunshine brings happiness. You are your own sunshine.

Loyalty is Deserving—
92. To win success in love you must cultivate sincerity and loyalty, and think a long while before marriage. Your love is of the lasting kind.

Conserve Magnetic Power—
93. Don't you know that men like bright, cheerful girls, and every ill-natured thought consumes your personal magnetism which you so very much need. Yes, you will attain wealth, love, friends and happiness.

Friendship Breeds Weariness—
94. Don't marry too young; you are naturally full of fancies. You lose your interest in people after you once win their regard.

Lacking in the Art of Attractiveness—
95. Don't run after men. Remember the hunted man generally vanishes.

Tactfulness—
96. You are too sentimental—too romantic—you have lost your chances. Keep a person of your choice interested; treat him as your equal; be chums, inspire him, jolly him along; men like to be jollied by lady admirers.

Rolling Stone Generally Goes Down Hill—

97. Stay at home; don't travel, it means a longer life for you.

Seek a Basis for Mutual Confidence—

98. Married life has ruined your happiness. Talk it over with him, he might mend his ways.

Trim Your Sails—

99. You can not make an ocean out of a thimbleful of water. Your ambition is abnormal.

Don't Wear Out Your Wings Flapping
Against the Boundaries of Your Sphere—

100. The ruination of most women is extravagance —trying to compete with millionairesses with a "thirty-cent" income. Be plain, neat, happy —it saves money and lots of tribulation.

NOTE:—If you intend to work birth months and lucky days you should request them to write the month in which they were born, and consult this list for suitable reply. This is the main part of the *Message Reading Act,* and which others fail to describe. It is a study by itself, and can be used for office or stage work.

USEFUL HINTS.

Don't feign mystery, that is—don't assume a mysterious air.

In answering questions, care should be taken not to destroy all hope. Of course, you cannot always picture only SUNSHINE, but the darkest picture should allow streaks of sunshine to break thru intermittently and more especially at the conclusion of your advice.

Question: Will my husband get better—should we sell out and go elsewhere?

Answer: Mrs. Marie Weeks: I get a strange vibration around you. Peculiar conditions exist with someone who is very near and dear to you. There is ill health

PRACTICAL TELEPATHY

—this I see changing for the better, and I see a party whom you are at present time worrying over, being once again well and happy.

Yes, I also see a sale. Not so soon, but a little later on it looks as though it would be the proper thing to do to go elsewhere. Yes, and you will find that better conditions will eventually come into your life.

Question: What month will I marry? Miss Kate M.

Answer: I see a little worry in your mind regarding life of "single blessedness." I see a man—a wonderful man, who speaks words of wisdom to you. I see you saying "Yes"—and that LITTLE WORD ALONE changes your entire future life, and in a short time, too. Of course, understand, I do not say positively that he will be happy, but I know you will be, and you are the one whose future I am advising.

A question like this: "When will I be married, and will I have any children?"—may be answered in the following fashion: Yes, I see you very happy in married life, and—listen! (Call her by first name). "THE HAND THAT ROCKS THE CRADLE, IS THE HAND THAT RULES THE WORLD," and you'll be busy rocking it (put up 6-7 fingers—meaning that she will be blessed with that many children). This always brings a laugh. A little wit is always appreciated in answering questions.

Here is a good stock question: "What is the matter with my FORD?" "What is the matter with my car—can it be fixed?"

Answer: I see an awful conglomerated mess in the crystal; it is hard for me to distinguish just what it is—Oh, yes! Now I see what it is. It is a tin Lizzie. There is something the matter with it, and you want me to tell you how to remedy it, but to be honest with you, I am a Seer and not a mechanic, and all I know about Fords is a lot of nutty stories.

A good one to pull off on the first night: For instance a question reads like this: "Does my sweetheart love me?" Mae Jones.

Answer: Mae Jones, where are you? Oh, there you are! You are anxious to know if your sweetheart loves you? Is that him with you now? If she says "Yes"—you say, "Well, I will find out for you. You rush down to them and take hold of their hands, and after a little thought, you say, "You bet he does—you have him right where you want him!"

Suppose a question like this: "Where can I find Gladys?" You say Mary Brown — or whatever the signed name may be—"You want to know about a friend. I don't quite see her name—you please concentrate on your friend's name for a second and I will try and get it. Oh! I have it—Gladys, isn't it?"

To the answer "Yes," you say. "I thought so."

(Note—This is a good way to dispose of test questions. At times some may just try to test you and by answering in this way you leave them in doubt.)

Another twist to use is: Call out a question and if the party doesn't answer, you say—"Now, John"—or whatever the name signed is—"if you don't answer me I will come down to your seat." This leaves a wonderful effect on the audience. In some instances, they will declare afterwards, that you actually went down to their seats.

Another dodge is this: Call the name, and pretend not to hear them. Note quickly the direction from which the voice comes from, and say: "Marie, you have written a question and now you refuse to acknowledge it, so I will have to come down to your seat. You rush down madly right to the seat, touch her (or him) on the shoulder and say, "You are Marie, etc." Such strategical maneuvers create a profound impression on the audience.

In answering questions, simulate great mental effort as though it taxed your psychic powers to the utmost. Never repeat a question word for word as it is written.

CHAPTER THREE

CHAPTER THREE

MIND READING

HISTORY OF MIND READING—CRYSTAL GAZING, SECOND SIGHT AND QUESTION ANSWERING ACTS.

Second sight was first performed by Pinetti in 1845. Robert Hiller got the idea from him and framed up a much stronger act than that of Pinetti's which he (Hiller) with his wife, performed with great success in conjunction with his TWO HORSE SHOW.

Houdin also performed this message or question answering, which was first performed on a stage by the noted Dr. Lynn. Prof. Hoffman, in his book. "More Magic," describes his performance of the folded message (billet) reading. (Strips of paper, on which questions were written by different spectators, which after being collected in a borrowed hat, were read and answered later upon the stage. Dr. Lynn did not make a complete act out of this, but performed it as a separate number in his lengthy performance.

Samri S. Baldwin (The White Mahatma), mentions the fact in his book that Charles Foster was the first to do MESSAGE READING as a "Medium" for office work. He was also the first to perform the weird but fascinating Blood Writing on the Arm effect.

Samri and his wife, Kitty Baldwin, were really the first performers to my knowledge to present a two or more hours entertainment with this in Opera Houses from two to five weeks in the larger cities. As far back as the eighties they toured the world, and ammassed a fortune. Baldwin was a master in this work; and in that pertaining to Spirit Cabinets. He spent a great deal of money investigating spiritualism, and his death at the age of eighty-two, robbed the world of one of the foremost entertainers in his particular branch of the arts.

Anna Eva Fay, (Mrs. John Pingill) who presented a two hour performance in Opera Houses with her husband years ago, offering Spirit Cabinet work in vaudeville acts, and closing the show with her question answering act, was another beacon light in this art. They copied the Baldwin method by watching the latter's performance until both were forced out of Opera House "time" by the formation of so many theatrical syndicates. Anna Eva Fay still plays vaudeville—always pulling the public with two-part performances.

"Eva Fay," who claims to be a relative of the "gifted one," is also appearing in vaudeville. Since the Crystal Gazing act has been presented, and with thousands of picture theatres all over the country, hundreds of camouflaged imitation "Hindu Seers" (?) have made their appearance—most of whom have made money, providing they possessed knowledge of what they were doing, experience and showmanship.

Clayton was the first to present it on an elaborate scale in the eastern part of the United States and abroad with success. Alla Axism, Alexander, Nolla Axmi, Marjah, Chandra (Harto) Zan-Zig, Canning, Daul, The Seer, Mehendrah, and many others too numerous to name them all, are performing the Crystal Gazing—Question Answering Act—mostly all using telephone wires, etc. Each have their own pet methods, but all using it in Hindu make-up. Where they get this Hindu idea from I don't know. Crystal gazing is not a new art or science. History tells us that it was practiced by the Egyptians 6,000 years before the Christian era.

Bome, the Hypnotist, performed a Hindu Crystal Gazing Act in 1896. The Zan-Zigs, Chandra (The Hartos), Nolla Axmi (The Wellers), have one advantage over others, as they are the only performers I know of in this line who really can transmit written questions

PRACTICAL TELEPATHY

correctly; doing away with all fakes. Back in the eighties, the Steenes were considered the best Second Sight artists. At the present time the Shanochs—(The Ellises), and Leona Lamar are the head liners in vaudeville. Others are presenting mind reading—thought transference acts in all branches of the show business.

Blackstone-Richards and other clever magicians have also added a Crystal Gazing Act to their performance,

PLANS, SCHEMES AND METHODS FOR OFFICE WORK.

The real money for somnolency (message reading), is in the daily office work or private reading engagements, providing the "seer" does not run a-foul of the law. You do not advertise your seances in the newspapers; but build

PLATE THREE

up a clientelle through the business and post card systems. You will readily find that a few "believers" will rush to your standard, and they, in turn, unconsciously become solicitors for other business. You can also announce from the stage at each performance that for those who wish SPECIAL or PRIVATE readings, your office hours are such and such.

My system has been that if they come in person and bring a card, it is fifty cents for three questions. On the other hand, if the card is sent to the hotel (my office) through the mail, the three questions will be answered and mailed back for twenty-five cents. The above applies only to general questions. It is always a rule to charge a special and higher fee when questions relative to "love," "business," etc., are involved.

I work and arrange my office at the hotel as follows:

A, the waithing or reception room; B, operating room; C, developing room; 1, 2, 3, are doors leading from hallway into each room; 4 and 5, are doors that connect the three rooms.

In the waiting or reception room be sure to have plenty of chairs for visitors. B, the operating room, has a table, a chair, some pads (not prepared), and some pencils. (If you prefer the sealed message system, use it, as explained elsewhere.) I use both the pads and the envelope method—both are good for this work.

The lady medium is in the developing room, where you have gold dust, plumbage, (lead dust) or bluing ready to develop questions. Lady also has some extra paper, and the stock questions ready. A, the reception room can be dispensed with entirely if rooms are upstairs. You may use the hotel parlors for this, also an usher in uniform who ushers them upstairs one at a time. It will be seen that two rooms with a door in between, will answer the purpose.

Don't let any one write over three questions. I always pretend that I am in a big hurry—look at my watch, act nervous and say that "my time is limited; others are waiting, so please hurry your questions. Write them on this pad while I leave the room. Tear off the sheet you write on, fold it up, hold it in your hand, place it in your purse, or hide it on your person." And "Madam," (or "Miss") "like the wireless Marconi System, will read your innermost thoughts. Write three questions."

I generally place pad in under their nose, and hand them a hard-pointed pencil and say: "Please write plain." There is also a tap bell on table, and I say: "When ready tap bell." I now leave room and enter developing room where madam stands ready; when bell rings I return to writer and right here is where I collect my fee 50c or $1.00, according as I think the prospects are.

I now tell her (or him): "I will tell the Madam that all is ready," but I am very careful to take the pad along with me into the developing room. As soon as I am under cover in next room, we both get busy developing the impressions left on paper, by rubbing gold dust or lead dust over it. It brings writing impressions out easily.

She now copies them on a piece of paper looks over her stock answers (which she should commit to memory). I always instruct the patrons to write their full name to messages.

Next, I introduce lady mind reader to writer, and for effect, blindfold her.

She now reads and answers the three questions *correctly!* The mystified customer is now ushered out by the professor. Our customer goes home, shows and reads her message to friends, relatives and neighbors, and they come to get THEIR MINDS READ TOO. In this manner all messages are read and answered.

Of course, if the theatre is convenient for this sort of thing, then it is a much better place than the hotel; where a crowd of noisy and wise transients usually are to be found.

PRACTICAL TELEPATHY

I prefer the envelope effect, but both the pad and envelope system should be as used, both are very practicable for this particular branch of the business. In small towns you can give one show a week; a matinee for ladies only, and announce the office business for after the show. Well worded ads—that will be of benefit to you—can be insterted in the newspapers without giving the address of your office. You can also play three nights and one week in good sized towns without fear of a "flop."

I would also suggest that you open with a thirty minute Spirit Cabinet Act; followed by two or three "hand bill" acts (not mystery), and close the performance with the message reading. Feature the lady in this, of course. Operate your office the last day in town. This has made good money for me.

A SIMPLE BUT EFFECTIVE MIND READING ACT AS PRESENTED BY PROF. ROBERT GIFFFORD.

EFFECT: Have your assistants distribute slips of paper for your audience to write their questions on. After the questions have been written, the assistants return to the stage with them, where they are placed on a tray and burned; the ashes being thrown away.

Next, you introduce your lady assistant, who sits in a chair, is covered with a sheet and proceeds to answer the questions a la Anna Eva Fay.

EXPLANATION: Briefly, the secret of this experiment consists of a Roterberg (or any other good make) changing bang and duplicate slips. The audience place their slips in the bag and by the time that the assistant has returned to the stage, the change has been made; the duplicates are burned and the bag thrown behind the wings. The genuine slips are then removed by the lady assistant and concealed about her person. Under the cover of the sheet she reads and answers them. If the stage is well lighted the questions can be easily read.

Answers to the questions, of course, depend entirely on what has been written. For instance ,if someone writes: "When will I be married?"—your answer would be—"As soon as you get the young lady's consent,"—in the case of a man, and—"As soon as the young man proposes to you,"—in the case of a woman.

On the other hand, suppose someone asks—"How much money have I in my pocket? Your answer could be—"You haven't any. You spent your last cent to come to the show," thereby securing comedy and passing over what might possibly be a embarassing issue should you attempt guess work in an effort to answer the question legitimately.

GENERAL MIND READING INCLUDING A NUMBER OF GOOD POINTS.

The following are some of my ideas along mind-reading, which I have listed because they have been found to be very practical:

Secure a metal ball, such as are used on the tops of flag-staffs, but not larger than seven inches in diameter, if possible. Open the ball, cut a small slit in its surface and insert a roller on pins, similar to the film roller in a kodak. Around this wind a strip of onion paper. The questions are written on the roller by the assistant and inserted in the ball. In apparently concentrating his attention on the globe, the performer simply reads the questions as he sees them through the slit, and answers them forwith. A small pivot should extend through the slit, to enable the performer to roll the strip, thereby bringing other questions into view. It is the same principle as the hand-box crystal.

Another method, which is considered easier, is to write the questions on paper and secure same to the wrist by means of a rubber band. Now, by holding the crystal in the same hand, you can read the question with ease. In this method, however, you run almost as much risk of detection as you do with the roller crystal, unless you are dexterious.

SUBSIDIZED HAT

A derby hat faked as a changing bag, is planted in the audience. One side holds the fake questions or blank slips. The questions are collected in the hat (which has previously been borrowed) by the assistant, who, on the way to the stage, turns the flap over, and dumps the fake questions on the performer's table. The hat is retained until after the performance "in case it might be needed again," thus giving the assistant an excuse to take same back stage to remove the genuine questions.

The questions, in turn, are removed from their envelopes and written on cards—or whatever the performer's method requires. One good method is to have them inserted in new envelopes with the answers and the writers' initials on the envelope as has been previously explained. These are secretly slipped to the performer by his assistant, while in the act of gathering up the questions on the table.

The performer now walks down among the audience with the envelopes in one hand and a pencil in the other; calls out the name, (seeing it on envelope) and, apparently writes his answer thereon merely bluffing, however, as the assistant has already done this.

In the act of gathering up the dummies from off the table they are either pressed through the trap or picked up in a handkerchief. The other questions are held together by a rubber band. In addressing the audience, the performer states that he has found that some of the questions were written before hand—at home—and that these are the ones which he will answer first. This, of course, gives the assistant ample time to fix up the real questions behind the scenes. These answers are usually given by the performer going among the audience.

Still another method is to have the answer written on the edge of the envelope. The performer calls the name of the person, tells what their question is, gives his answer and then tears open the envelope and withdraws the question. In so doing he tears off the portion that has the writing.

MENTAL X-RAY

Instead of a crystal ball, demonstrate your power of mental pentration by securing a METAL GLOBE from an optician—such as are used in window displays. These are better than glass as the audience cannot see through them, which is often convenient when using the "hand box."

PALMISTRY.

At an "off" moment, a time when the assistant is engaged in "straightening" up the stage after a series of experiments, the performer steps behind the wings, and quickly writes the questions on the palm of his hand. Only a limited number can be put on of course, and these must be abbreviated. By this method the art of answering questions is reduced to "no art" at all. If using the crystal ball, simply hold the ball on the palm and read the questions right through it. It is not necessary to lay stress upon the fact that as only a limited number of questions can be written on the hand, this method is effective only when used in conjunction with another.

SOMNOLENCE AND MESSAGE READING AS PERFORMED BY PROF. HELM.

Being in this line of business for years, I am naturally familiar with every known method of mind-reading. Anna Eva Fay and others advertise that people may write their questions at home and bring them to the theatre or write them on their own paper. As yet, I have never seen any of these questions answered. They are always passed up. With Prof. Helm's forthcoming message, this can actually be accomplished.

EFFECT: The billing reads that people may write their questions on their own paper and at home. At the performance, performer announces: "If people have not written their questions at home they may do so now on their own paper; but for the convenience of those who have no paper or pencil, he will furnish same—which he does—no fake. He requests people to write their full name and questions that can be described to a mixed audience; that all improper or objectionable questions will be passed up entirely.

He now gives a large decorated box for close inspection—NOT prepared. He next requests some prominent man to select a committee of four or more to collect the messages in their own hats; which they do, and once more the box is shown and the messages are now placed in the box by the committee.

The professor takes the box on the stage and plaecs it on an ordinary kitchen table. (Not prepared). He now shows another box just like it, proves it empty and proceeds to mix the messages by dumping them from one box to another, leaving them on the table in one of the boxes, he slides the other box off stage out of the way. He now erects on the stage, in plain view of audience, a cloth cabinet; the front has a circular gauze, transparent opening. A small table with a lighted candle, (electric light can be used instead) on it, and a chair is also placed inside of cabinet The lady is now introduced—gallatan make-up, hair down loose—made up full for effect. She is looking upward and is constantly murmuring to herself, (for effect). Music "Ben Bolt." She takes her seat in the cabinet, curtain closed. Spectators can see her inside by light inside. Megaphone on rack now placed in front with mouthpiece leading inside of cabinet.

Performer now takes each message out from box, holds it high above his head, and the lady first calls the writer by name and reads the message and answers it correctly, and in a clear and distinct voice thru the megaphone. In this manner he takes up 12 to 30 minutes.

Lady also makes predictions on weather and crops, also baseball and sporting events; describes some deceased person; names the relatives, who are perhaps among the audience. Writes of lost friends and relatives, and so forth. Many other effects can be worked with ease, limited only by the knowledge and skill of the performer. This method is in a class all by itself and really does what others advertise, but never put across.

EXPLANATION: The real secret is in the second box (not the one which was examined). The kitchen table has drapery around it and this trick box is concealed below the table. It really is not concealed. Here is an illustration of it.

A and B, two separate compartments. In A there are a bunch of duplicate folded messages which the performer has put there beforehand. Compartment B is empty. C is a sliding lid that slides from A to B.

After the performer comes on the stage with the other box, (the one that has been examined), which has the real messages in it, he places it on the table, and the trick box with the concealed fake messages inside it is brought to view from beneath table. He shows the inside—it is painted a dead black. He shows the outside is decorated. (Both boxes look alike). He now announces that he will mix the messages to prove that he uses no confederates among the audience. The mixing should be done so that the trick box should come below on table at third movement, with real messages in trick box; these are now all all crowded into compartment B — the vacant part. The lid, C, is slid over them and this time the fake messages are dumped into the unprepared box. The movement is natural. The audience imagine they are the same messages. The trick box with the real messages inside is now slid behind scenes in a careless way, where lady stands ready. She slides lid to other side,

PRACTICAL TELEPATHY

takes messages out of box and places them into a small sack. This bag has two compartments. Top has a hem thru which runs a strong cord long enough so that the lady can tie it around one of her legs.

While she is doing all this, the professor is setting up the cabinet in plain view of audience. This cabinet has no frame work, but is sawed in one square piece; has a ring on each corner to which are snapped, with snap hooks, four guy lines leading from fore part of stage thru screw eyes. This is all fixed beforehand so that all we have to do is to snap on the four hooks so that bottom part of cabinet nearly touches the floor. The table with lighted candle or electric light is now placed inside, also the chair. The lady is now introduced, as already explained. Audience can see her thru the circular, transparent guaze front, that is they imagine they can see her, only the upper part of her body. There is an extra opening in front of curtain for mouthpiece and megaphone to go thru. As the professor is arranging and explaining this, the lady reaches down and unties the bag from leg, opens it and holds it in her lap.

Professor now explains that he will take out each message separately still folded, and hold it high above his head. Sometimes I call a little girl on the stage to take the messages out from the box, hand them to me (one at a time, of course). When I say ready for the first, lady deliberately reads it by the light inside of cabinet. When I want her to know that I am holding the next one, I say "Next," and in this manner she first calls the writer by name, then hesitates and professor says: "Please hold up your hand;" he now knows that the party who has been called is really there. The lady then proceeds to read the message and puts a suitable answer to all questions in a clear voice through the suspended megaphone. As soon as the lady finishes with answering a message, she places it in the corner of the bag in the other compartment, and in this manner from twelve to fifteen questions can be handled in short order.

EXACT QUESTIONS AND ANSWERS OF COUNT CHILO AND MABELLE; TAKEN DOWN IN SHORTHAND BY GEORGE BERRY, IN 1914. AN EXCELLENT INSIGHT INTO QUESTION ANSWERING.

Question: Well, see whether you can answer this if you please, Madam.

Answer: This person wants to know regarding a certain piece of property which is covered by a mortgage. It seems to me this will be paid within the next five years.

Question: What has this gentleman on his mind?

Answer: Absolutely nothing, professor.

Question: Come on; tell me about this, please, quick.

Answer: You want to know about your position— (hesitatingly).

Question: Concentrate your mind on this, Madam. (To audience), Madam cannot keep her mind on the question.

Answer: I see a strike where this gentleman is employed. It will be settled within the next five weeks, in favor of the employees.

Question: Answer this, please, tell about this.

Answer: You ask regarding your sister. She will get well if she can possibly get the change of climate.

Question: Now answer this, this lady's question.

Answer: It seems to me this lady is thinking of making a change of residence. You will like your new home.

Question: Get your mind on this.

Answer: I don't see a move for you for the next eight months.

Question: Can you answer this, please? Can you answer this question?

Answer: You ask regarding your father; he will probably get well. I would advise a change of climate.

Question: You answer this, if you please, come on.

Answer: It is in regard to. . . . It seems to me that he would do better with present partner.

Question: Answer this, if you please.

Answer: I would advise you to be a moving picture operator. I see success for you in that line.

Question: Now answer this, please, this ladies.

Answer: This lady is contemplating a change of residence. You will not like the new place. You will only stay there a month. I see another change after that.

Question: Right. I want you to answer this here, please. Get your mind on it.

Answer: You want to know regarding the gentleman you are going with, if he is married. This gentleman has been married at one time, but his wife is dead.

Question: Answer this here, if you please; come on, get busy!

Answer: Your husband is contemplating a change in his position. I think it would be advisable to make the change.

Question: Now try and answer this, this lady's.

Answer: This lady wants to know how long she will stay in her present residence. She will stay there another year.

Question: Get your mind on this here question.

Answer: Within the next seven months you will make a change. You will go on a farm, but you won't like it.

Question: Do you know the answer to this? Answer this question.

Answer: You want to know regarding your sweetheart, (did not get the rest of answer).

Question: See whether you can answer this, can you? Quick, Madam.

Answer: This gentleman wants to know regarding his mother. I think she is in Pennsylvania. You will hear from her very soon.

Question: I want you to try and answer this if you please. (Get your mind on this. ??—?)

Answer: Next month you will get a raise of $1.00.

Question: That is right. Put your mind on this question, Madam.

Answer: You ask regarding your marriage. I do not see any marriage for you, for the next ten years. You are too young to think of love affairs.

Question: Get your mind on this here.

Answer: It seems to me you will only hold your new position four months You will change and go to another state. It seems to be the State of Nebraska.

Question: Tell me about this, please, quick.

Answer: Well, he wants to know if he will get certain news. It seems to me that he will.

Question: Say how soon.

Answer: Within the next three days.

Question: I want you to answer this, Madam, quick.

Answer: It seems you are contemplating a change in position. I would not advise you to make the change you have in mind.

Question: Now answer this.

Answer: You want to know regarding your husband. He will get along all right with his partner.

Question: Tell about this, now Madam, question.

Answer: You want to know how long you will stay here. You will stay two months and then you go East.

Question: Yes, answer this man's question.

Answer: He wants to know regarding success in business. It seems to me you will be a little disappointed at first, but later on, it will prove satisfactory.

Question: Your mind on this, if you please, Madam.

PRACTICAL TELEPATHY

Answer: In the next nine days you will get a position.

Question: Answer this, if you please, this lady's question.

Answer: She wants to know regarding her father—how he came to his death. It seems to me it was thru an accident.

Question: See if you can answer this, if you please.

Answer: It is regarding a certain piece of property. You want to know if oil will be found in it. Yes, oil will be found there in large quantities.

Question: Yes, get your mind on this, if you please.

Answer: I would advise you to make the change you are contemplating.

Question: That is quite right, answer this, if you please.

Answer: You want to know regarding a piece of property, regarding the sale of it. I would advise you to hold it for another year; there will be a raise in the value of it.

Question: Well, answer this, please. Tell me about this one.

Answer: Your sister will get well.

Question: I want you to try and answer this, if you please, Madam.

Answer: You want to know how long you will stay at your present employment. It seems to me you will stay there 14 more months.

Question: Tell me about this, if you please.

Answer: It is regarding a letter. It seems to be from your brother. It won't contain very good news. You will be disappointed.

Question: Well, that's right, answer this.

Answer: You want to know regarding a certain sum of money. You will get the money in small installments.

CHAPTER FOUR

PRACTICAL TELEPATHY

CHAPTER FOUR

THE GREAT POWERS' FAMOUS MIND READING ACT IN FIVE DIVISIONS AS DESCRIBED PROF. POWERS.

To begin with it is necessary to pick out the most fluent and capable speaker in your troupe to act as talker or caller in the audience, while the less gifted orator remains on the stage to act as medium. Both medium and talker must know how to receive and send messages. Therefore, it requires considerable practice to become fluent and perfect and familiar with all the cues, as all cues must be answered without hesitation before attempting to appear before an audience. Furthermore, it must be borne in mind that after you become acquainted with this act it will require constant practice to keep yourself in trim.

FIRST DIVISION.

You must learn the alphabet from A to Z. You must know where every letter belongs from A to Z by number; 1 to 26, so you can call any number rapidly and have the medium give you the desired letter. Also be able to call any letter and have him give you the number; for example; No. 17 equals Q; 23, W; 7, G, etc. Do the same with letters; K, 11; Y, 25; M, 13, etc.

SECOND DIVISION.

Pass words:

Audience stands for	A or	1
Be	B or	2
Can or Can't	C or	3
D or Don't	D or	4
Fix	E or	5

PRACTICAL TELEPATHY

```
Figure or Letter_____F or  6
Give _____G or  7
Have _____H or  8
I _____I or  9
One snap with the fingers stands for___J or 10
Two snaps with the fingers stands for__T or 20
```

Supposing you wish to send E or 5, say to Medium: "Fix your mind on this letter; what is it?" Naturally it will be E as password, "Fix" stands for letter E.

Supposing you wish to send G or 7, say, "Give me this letter." Give stands for letter G or 7. Supposing you wish to send M, which is 13, you will say, "Can you tell this letter?" And snap your fingers ONCE as you do so; C stands for 3, being the third letter and one snap means 10; 10 plus 3 equals 13, and 13 is M. We will suppose you wish to send R, it would be one snap plus: "Let me have this letter." "Have" is 8, and one snap is 10; 10 plus 8 is 18, and 18 is R. Suppose you wish to send W, you would say: "Can you tell this letter?" and snap your fingers twice. "Can" is 3, and two snaps 20; 20 plus 3 equals 23, or W. Always make up your letter or number by the password plus snap or snap alone or password alone, such as the case may be. Supposing you wish to send F cue: "What letter is this?" "Letter" is F. Supposing you wish to send No. 6 cue: "What figure is this?" "Figure" is 6. Supposing you wish to send J; ask the question and use one snap which equals 10 or J, but be sure you don't use any passwords in your questions, as it would bring different results. Supposing you wish to send "7". Use two snaps, which equals 20—use no passwords.

Now it will happen that the caller makes a mistake and makes a miscall which he does not notice until it is too late; in such cases interrupt the medium by saying: "Now don't get nervous; rest your mind a moment." Repeat the desired cue correctly; the medium instantly is informed of the error in this way unknown to the audience as the words: "Rest your mind" are the error cue. It will also happen that the medium does not catch the cue sometimes on account of the noise in the audience; in such cases he will say to the caller, "I can't make it out; there seems to be a dark vision before me."

The caller is now informed that he did not hear it and he repeats the cue. The medium must always read the *first* cue in the conversation as the other cues that are sometimes brought in do not mean anything; therefore the caller must bring it to a point to use his one word on or near the opening of his question to avoid mistakes as the second password does not count except in compound cues. This you will get later.

Now, don't study any further until you can execute the above with lightning rapidity and perfect accuracy.

THIRD DIVISION.

We are now ready to start and send messages, so we will start with the coin test. First of all, we will blindfold the medium and have him seated facing the audience. The medium should be 20 or 30 feet from the caller in rehearsals so he will form the habit of listening closely.

When you have made a study of division one and two, you will have the key to the entire system. All you will need now is the different tables the letters stand for. He will always know what table you have reference to as he can tell that by the question.

COIN TEST.

Cue—"What's in my hand," means a copper coin.

Cue—A for 1 cent—B for 2c.

Cue—"Tell us," means a nickel.

No value necessary.

Cue—"What's this," means a silver coin.

There are four pieces of silver in a dollar. A is 10c, B is 25c, C is 50c, D is $1.00.

Send with the above letters.

PRACTICAL TELEPATHY

First send the cue for material, then the value, and last the date.

Cue—"I am deeply obliged," means a gold coin.

A is $1.00, B is $2.50, Fix is $5.00, 1 snap is $10.00, two snaps is $20.00. Send above letters for value.

Example: Supposing I receive a silver half dollar; I would say: "What's this?" Medium would answer, "It comes to me as a silver coin." Next, I would say: "Can you tell the value of it?" Can is C, and C stands for 50c. Next, I would call the date; if the date is previous to 1890 call each figure separately, but if it is from 1890 to our present date, we send the cue in one word. 1890 no password and no snap. For anything in between these dates, use password only. 1900 is 1 snap, no password. For anything between these dates, 1 snap and password. 1910, 2 snaps, no password. Over this date use two snaps and password.

Example: Say 1890 is wanted, "What's the date?"

Answer: 1890.

Say 1897 is wanted.

Cue: "Give me the date."

Answer: 1897.

Say 1913 is wanted.

Cue: "Can you tell the date?" And snap fingers twice; C is 3 and two snaps 20; 20 plus 3 are 23, and 23 is 1913. So you will easily understand how you can get these dates. It is very simple after you practice a while. Now, the party may wish to have you ask the medium where this coin comes from; then use these cues: A stands for U. S.; C for Canadian of chimes; M for Mexican. Send E for foreign coins. For all foreign coins outside of the above stated send E.

Suppose you receive a paper bill, a check or paper certificate of any kind; you must say to spectator, "Much Obliged;" that means you have received a paper certificate of some kind. If it is a paper bill, say to Medium: "What is it, a check?" Medium answers: "It is a paper bill."

If you receive a check, say to Medium: "What is it, a bill?" Medium answers: "It is a check." It is always the reverse from what you ask.

On bills call value thus: $1 is A, $2 is B, $5 is Fix, $10 use one snap and no password. Now on checks use compound cues, for example: The amount is $47.28—cue would be: "DON'T make a mistake and give me this amount of dollars this check calls for." Now, we put these cues together. D equals 4 and C is 7, thus we have 47 answer; call the cents in the same way.

Call the serial number of check and paper bill one number at a time. If you should have to read a naught (0) read it thus: "And the next?" If the check calls for $30.44, send it thus: Cue: "Can you tell the number of dollars this checks calls for? Come! Come! Come!" C is 3 and "Come! Come! Come!" means naught (0) in this case. Answer would be $30.00. Now, we want the CENTS, so we say, Cue: "Don't make a mistake and tell me the number of cents; Hurry up!" Answer, 44 cents. Don't is D or 4, and "Hurry up!" means to repeat, so answer is two 4's or 44.

FOURTH DIVISION.

Now, we have an article system which is as follows:

A. A tooth pick.
B. A boy.
B. H. A bald head.
C. A comb.
C. A. A card of any kind.
C. H. A check (not a bank check).
D. A handkerchief.
E. A pair of eye glasses.
F. A fountain pen.
G. A glove.
H. A hat
I. A match.

J. Jewelry (brooch, bracelet or locket only).

There are always two cues for jewelry; send these in separate calls. First, send J for jewelry, then in second call send the desired piece of jewelry. Thus: O for brooch, B for bracelet, L for locket.

K. A knife.
L. A lead pencil.
M. A mirror.
P. A purse.
S. A shirt.
Q. A pin of any kind.
T. A necktie.
N. Means nothing; good to fool audience.
O. A button or badge emblem.

Send letter in second call to identify lodge.

R. A ring (send initial and color of stone in calls to follow).
U. A hairpin.
V. A button hook.
W. A waist.
X. A match box.
Y. A key.

Now in sending a fountain pen or a purse you have to make two, thus: For a fountain pen, cue: "What LETTER would you use to spell this article?" Medium: "I would use F." Caller: "What would you call the article?" Medium: "A fountain pen."

Ask question on purse the same way, only use one snap to make it P for No. 16. Medium answers the same way, only answer in this case would be a purse.

MISCELLANEOUS CUES.

A pipe; cue: "What does this smell like?"
Answer: "A sewer—Oh, no!—I mean a pipe.
A cigar; cue: "What would you do if you had this?"

Answer: "I would smoke it." Caller: "What is it?"
Answer: "It comes to me as a cigar."

A cigarette; cue: "What do you think of this?"

Answer: "It comes to me as a bundle of hay wrapped in paper—Oh, no!—I mean a cigarette."

Souvenier; cue: "When does this gentleman trust me with?"

In case an article is forced on the caller for which he has no cue, take it and call thus: "What's this? What's this? Come."

Medium answers: "There is a dark vision before me, I can't make it out." Return the article to the party stating that you will get him later; but by all means don't go near him again—forget him. Always try and avoid calling articles for which you have no cue, as you have your own choice of articles.

FIFTH DIVISION.

We will close the act by the watch test. Here the caller is supposed to make a strong spiel boosting the medium as it will help wonderfully on the close. Now ask for a time piece. Of course, the medium already knows what you have, so you don't have to ask him. First ask what the case consists of: For gold send G; for silver send S; for gun metal send M.

Next we want the movement:

A. For American movement.
E. For Elgin movement.
H. For Hampton movement.
I. For Ingersoll movement.
R. For Rockford movement.
S. For Swiss movement.
W. For Waltham movement.

I think these will be all you need as nearly every watch

you run across is either of these movements. If you get a movement you have no call for—don't call it.

Next, we want the correct time. The medium should always post himself on the hour he is working in as the minutes are only sent in the compound cues as in the amount of a check. Say the time is 8:28; cue would be: "Be sure and let me have the correct time;" being 8:28.

Should the man's watch be stopped or away out of time—then ask for the hour of the watch and minutes later. Send 11th and 12th hour by snap. Cue: Not compound. Give number of jewels next. If below 20 use snap cue. If above 20, use compound cue. Send initials, if any.

Now hurry back on stage and close with short speech.

In case a watch is forced on you before time, cue would be: "I am now going to give you something difficult." Don't read the watch; leave it to finish the act with.

I think you will find plenty of cues in the act to cover all the ground you wish to, and I will give you my best wishes for success. But, remember you must work accurately and rapidly; and the caller must keep moving among the audience. The faster you work, the more you baffle the audience; as the moment you let yourself "drag" some of your spectators will immediately begin attempting to trip you up. You can call the cues I have given you in any way you wish, as there is no fixed routine. The medium always knows what is coming, by the conversation.

CHAPTER FIVE

PRACTICAL TELEPATHY

CHAPTER FIVE

SEANCES, SECOND SIGHT AND SPECIALTY EFFECTS AND EXPERIMENTS FOR THE MEDIUM.

THE SEANCE.

PERFORMANCE: The performer first passes for inspection three brass hoops, each about six inches in diameter. These are separate, not linked. He next brings forth a blank visiting card, an opaque envelope, a bottle of India ink, pen, piece of sealing wax and a lighted candle.

A spectator is then requested to write four short questions on the card or paper. Upon the performer's request the spectator places the card in the envelope, written side up, whereupon it is securely closed with the sealing wax.

The attention of the audience is now called to 13 tumblers on a table; each filled with clear water. The following are also on the table: slate, slate pencil, bell, pistol (loaded with blank), tambourine, wine-glass (containing either wine or water), and a piece of one-quarter inch rope two feet long. The rope is now brought out and the performer has it marked and requests the audience to tie any number of knots in it. This is placed on the table together with the sealed envelope and the rings.

The performer is now tied to a chair by the committee and placed near the table. A screen is set in front of him and almost at once, the bell commences to ring, the tambourine to rattle, etc., all of which are eventually thrown over the screen. The piece of rope follows shortly, and it is seen that the knots have been untied.

PRACTICAL TELEPATHY

After a few moments silence, strains of weird but sweet music permeate the audience. (This is played on the 13 glasses and will be described further on). This is immediately followed by the performer's coat.

The rings are heard rattling and also the sound of writing on the slate. Suddenly comes the roar of the pistol being fired, followed instantly by the weapon itself being thrown over the secreen; which is then withdrawn by the assistant.

The performer is still seated and bound to the chair, a ring over each arm and the third ring LINKED between. On the table are the 13 glasses but in place of water they now contain various colored wine; for example—the glasses being in a row—the contents of the center glasses being red, white and blue while that of the glasses on either side can be varied. The wine glass which originally contained wine or water is now found to be empty.

Upon examining the slate—which was originally blank —it is found to contain the four questions that were written on the card, (with answers in the envelope). The envelope is then returned untampered with. On the floor is the rope—untied! Also the coat, pistol, tambourine and bell.

Explanation: You have a set of 6 rings, altho the audience only sees three at a time. Each ring is solid enough but three are *linked together*. (If you have a set of linking rings you can use two unprepared ones and also the two linked ones. I have suggested three as it is more effective). The three separate ones are hid in the place where you have the linked ones concealed. A good place to hide these are in a special pocket made in the portion of the table cover which hangs down. Arrange the linked rings correctly before replacing hands.

To color the water have the following dyes concealed. A small quantity of lime, red, blue, and yellow. To make the different colors—Red, drop in red dye; blue, drop in blue dye; yellow, drop in yellow dye; green, drop in

PRACTICAL TELEPATHY

yellow and add blue slowly until the required shade is produced; purple, red first and add blue slowly until the required shade is produced; brown, yellow and blue to make a light green, then add red until the required shade is attained; pink, a small quantity of red; sky blue, small quantity of blue; pea-green, yellow and blue (only a very small quantity of blue); white, small quantity of lime (not too much as it settles).

SECOND SIGHT THAT'S OUT OF SIGHT.

The performer places three ordinary dice on a slate or tray and his assistant takes them among the audience, allowing anyone to throw the dice; whereupon the performer immediately announces the sum total of the spots uppermost.

EXPLANATION: The least anyone can throw is three (3 aces), and the most is 18 (3 sixes). The code, therefore, consists of 16 signals as follows:

The assistant holds the tray with both hands and if number three is thrown the assistant continues to hold the tray with both hands.

If the sum total is five, his left arm hangs by his side with fist closed.

When six is thrown the left hand rests on the hip at the fork of the thumb, thumb pointing behind, with fingers to the front.

If the amount thrown is seven, the left loose fist rests on the hip, fingers and thumb pointing behind.

When the throw is eight the assistant puts his left hand into his pocket.

On nine, he casually places his left arm behind him.

Ten is conveyed to the performer, by the assistant taking hold of the lapel of his coat with his left hand.

When eleven is thrown his right hand hangs by his side (holding tray with the left).

The only variation of the code on twelve is that the right hand fist closes.

For thirteen the right hand rests on the hip at fork of thumb; with the fingers pointing forward and the thumb behind.

When fourteen is thrown the right fist rests on the hip with fingers and thumb pointing behind.

On fifteen the performer casually slips his right hand into his trousers' pocket.

For sixteen the right hand is placed behind the back.

To signal seventeen the assistant takes hold of his right lapel with his right hand.

The tray is held on the palm of the right hand when eighteen is thrown.

ADDITIONAL POINTERS.

The assistant should always hold the tray with both hands when the dice are being thrown. He can then release it with one hand according to the requirements of the signals. Should the assistant's right side be toward the performer when eleven is thrown, and the next throw should be six, the assistant must take care not to be in too big a hurry to turn around; but should wait long enough for the thrower of the dice to figure up the result of the throw. In the meantime, however, the assistant lets go of the tray with his left hand so that the performer will know that the signal will come from the left side, and, therefore, will wait until the assistant makes the turn.

Each time that the assistant has occasion to turn around he should immediately request someone on that side of the aisle or room, which he is now facing, to throw the dice. (This furnishes a plausible reason for his having turned around). As soon as the performer announces the result of a throw, the assistant should take hold of the tray with both hands.

In the case of a lady assistant, the signals can be easily arranged; for instance, should the lady have no pockets in her costume, when eight or fifteen are thrown, she can take hold of her skirt and turn her hand over. Twelve to fourteen throws are sufficient. Devote twenty minutes a day to practising this effect and the result in a short time will surprise you.

SEALED ENVELOPE MYSTERY.
For Public Seances.

I work this experiment in conjunction with others in the following manner:

An assistant is previously planted in the audience. Slips of paper are then distributed for some test or other. In addition to this, four other slips and the same number of envelopes are distributed to four members of the audience; it being imperative that one of them being near where the assistant sits, so that when the questions are collected he (the assistant) will secure an envelope.

The four members of the audience write their respective questions, seal them and place them in a hat, while I am collecting the other slips which are not sealed. During these maneuvers the assistant gets hold of one of these envelopes and when I come to him he drops the envelope in the hat with the other three. I then ask him, casually, if he has signed his name to the question to which he replies, "No."

I request that he remove it from the hat, open it and place his name on it and I give him a new envelope in which to seal the question. (It of course does not matter which question he takes from the hat, as his duty is simply to find out what is written on one of the slips written by the four people. While he is "correcting his error" I go right on collecting the other slips. In the meantime the assistant reads the question and writes it on the envelope which he has torn open; after which he slips the original question in the new envelope and seals it. Upon my return he drops the envelope in the hat with the other questions, where it remains on top. Care should be taken to keep track of this envelope.

PRACTICAL TELEPATHY

In the meantime the assistant has given me the torn envelope which I have placed on top of the blank ones in my hand, and in going back to the table, I turn it over and read the question. In pouring the envelopes and questions out on the table, I keep track of the question envelope. After a preliminary reading of a couple of other slips, I pick up the envelope (the contents of which I know) and, holding it high in the air say: "I see a bright light over the lady's (or gentleman's) head. (Previous knowledge of the order in which the envelopes were placed in the hat makes it possible for me to know to whom it belongs).

Walking slowly over to her (or him) I hold the envelope over her head for a moment and then hand it to her. After a moment of apparent concentration I slowly recite the message aloud, giving the best answer I can and leave the envelope with the spectator. In nine times out of ten it is torn open, and the question passed around to those sitting near.

This experiment is so bewildering in its effect that the audience thinks nothing of my not reading the contents of the other three envelopes. Following this I proceed to continue in my reading of the slips on the table. The above is one of my finest effects for reputation creation and to puzzle the "wise heads" in the audience who are acquainted with carbon, wax pads, etc.

CHAPTER SIX

CHAPTER SIX

MIND READING AND MENTAL TELEPATHY IN WHICH SLATES PREDOMINATE.

THE BLACKBOARD.

The secret of this amazing experiment lies solely in the use of a small mirror which the blindfolded lady (preferably) assistant holds in her right hand. She sits facing the audience and is blindfolded in such a manner as to allow her slight vision beneath it. Her arms are raised before her with the hands crossed at the breast, making it possible to look downward into the mirror and see just what transpires to the left, right and rear back of her for a considerable radius. More territory can, of course, be brought into focus, by slight movement of the mirror hand either way.

The performer should have a large black-board standing on the stage in back and a little to the left of where the "medium," "Madam," or subject is seated. Near the black-board is placed a small stand on which is a deck of cards and a piece of chalk. Blindfolded in the manner described above, the "accomplice" sits in a chair near the foot-lights facing the audience.

"I invite anyone to step on the stage and to write a series of figures: say six wide and six deep, on this blackboard."

That is your general statement to all. Pick up the piece of chalk and aside from requesting the spectator to make the figures large enough for all to see them, you remain very quiet.

When this is accomplished and the spectator has retired, pick up the piece of chalk and await for your assistant to begin. At no time do you say a word, for

PRACTICAL TELEPATHY

fear that the audience may deduct that you are using a verbal code, of which there are thousands in existence today.

The assistant begins by adding the columns lengthwise, you writing down the totals as she calls them out. They are next added crosswise. You can touch any figure at random and immediately the blindfolded woman will call out what the number is. Innumerable other oddities can be performed such as touching a part of the black-board on which there is nothing written, as though attempting to confuse your confederate; but she instantly says— "There is nothing there."

You now request someone else to step up on the stage. Hand them the pack of cards with the request that they shuffle them well, and spread them out on the table in two rows, face up, picking up any card they wish or several cards. As soon as the spectator has retired, stand back of the table and pick up the cards one at a time. Hold them up so that all can see them, and in doing this give your assistance also sufficient time to get their reflection through the mirror. It will give the experiment considerable additional strength if, in reading or naming off the cards, the assistant uses a line of patter, similar to the following:

"I see what seems to be a red card. Yes, it is red . . . . It is a heart. . . . . The nine of hearts. Now. . . . . I see a black card. . . . a black face card. . . . . It is the Jack of spades." This is all done in a slow, hesitant manner on the part of the assistant.

There are various methods of concealing the mirror. In the case of a lady assistant, it might be permanently attached to a fan, or concealed in a handkerchief. In any event it should not be more than an inch and a half or two inches in diameter.

By experimenting beforehand, you can easily tell just where to place the black-board, chair and stand. If the engagement is for several days, it might be well to insure yourself against a hitch-up, by marking the stage on the exact spot where each thing stands.

Although very simple to read in explanation, the above method is far more baffling than many of the expensive mechanical and code secrets offered for sale. In most instances of this kind, the audience is always on the lookout for some manner of signals.

MALY'S BOOK AND SLATE MYSTERY.

EFFECT: Several books are handed to a spectator with the request that he make a selection of one. A school slate is also shown, cleaned thoroughly on both sides, and finally tied up in a borrowed handkerchief, whereupon it is given to someone to hold. Next a pack of cards is shuffled after the court (face cards) have been removed from the pack.

The pack is now fanned by the performer, back up to the spectator, who is requested to remove a card but not to look at it. The pack is then squared up and laid on the table. The spectator is asked to cut the pack in two equal halves—or as nearly so as possible—and select one of them. (This is not a "forced" selection). The performer now counts off ten cards from the selected half of the deck, giving the spectator preference as to whether they shall be counted from the top or bottom. (This is another instance wherein it makes no difference whether cards are counted from top or bottom). The "pips" or spots on these ten cards are now counted and whatever their total may be, the person holding the book is asked to open it at the page corresponding to the number of "pips." The performer then requests the party holding the card to look at it and tell the audience. We will say that it is the Ten of Spades. The person holding the book counts down to the tenth word on the page and states what it is. Upon removing the handkerchief from the slate, the word is found to be clearly written thereon.

PREPARATION: Arrange the deck a la "Si Stebbins" and remove the court cards—bridging them, and allowing them to remain on top of the pack. Now take two books and after deciding which one you wish to use, turn to page 55, and count down to the tenth word, and write same on the slate covering it with the "flap." (I always use a Thayer Midget Slate) enabling me to get rid of the "flap" by demonstrating how convenient it is to carry a slat of this size in the pocket.

PRESENTATION: Come forward with two books, one in each hand. Ask a spectator to touch either book. (I find that nine times out of ten it is the book in the left hand which is the prepared volume). I then put the book not chosen aside and proceed. Should by any chance the book in the right hand be chosen, lay it aside and remark: "We have no further use for this one then"—It is simply the old "gag" of elimination. The slat is then introduced and wiped on both sides with a handkerchief.

Dispose of the "flap" by any method which you may prefer, providing it is not too apparent to the spectators, and after wrapping the slate in a handkerchief, hand it to someone to hold. Pick up the deck and, after cutting them at the bridge, give them a "dove-tail" shuffle and bring the court cards into the body of the pack. This does not, in any way, alter the arrangement of the cards. Inform the audience that the court cards must be eliminated and proceed to remove them. Be very careful in doing this that you do not disturb the arrangement of the deck. Appear to look through the deck to be sure that all face cards have been removed, and while doing so manage to cut the deck at a TEN SPOT on any suit. This should be brought to the center (by means of the pass) and forced on someone. When the card is selected, be sure to transfer all cards that were above the TEN SPOT, to the bottom of the pack, so that the cards are in regular order again. The cards are then returned to the table, cut in halves and one of the halves selected (either one). Then proceed to count ten cards from either the top or the bottom of the selcted pile, as the audience may decide. It does not make any difference as the total of the "pips" on the ten cards will always be 55 unless, of course, a mistake has been made somewhere in the previous arrangement of them. The balance of the experiment follows in subsequent order as explained above.

It is possible to do away with the forcing of the TEN SPOT on a member of the audience by resorting to the elimination process. Ask a spectator to think of two out of three numbers FIVE, TEN or FIFTEEN. If he thinks of FIVE and FIFTEEN, simply declare that it leaves TEN and that is the number you will use. If he takes FIVE and TEN, then ask him to think of one of them. Should he say TEN, all well and good, use it. If his final selection is FIVE, say "that leaves TEN," and use it. It is not necessary to go into the elimination process here, as it is so commonly known to all performers with any experience whatsoever.

THE CHALKED SLATE TEST.

This illusion is one of the achievements of Edward Earl, a wonder-worker of the Pacific Coast. He is, perhaps, one of the cleverest if not THE cleverest "fakers" of the west. The apparatus for this experiment can be procured at a stationery store at a very nominal cost.

The requirements are as follows:

First: Two small school slates. Second: A slicate slab or flap that will fit snugly—but not tight—into the frame of one of the slates. Third: An ordinary newspaper. Fourth: A slate pencil, a piece of chalk or crayon, a towel and a glass of water.

Should you not be near a magic depot, the silicatce flap can be quickly secured at any stationery store by buying a large "book slate" and cutting out and fitting one of the leaves. This flap should be covered on one side with a piece of newspaper by glueing it down tightly all over the entire surface.

In my performance of this effect I use a slab made of

regular slate, making it possible then, to hold the slates under the very noses of my spectators without fear of their detecting the subtefuge. It takes a great deal of time and patience to grind the real slate flap to the required size, but the result is worth the trouble.

On one of the slates draw a diagonal chalk line from corner to corner. Do the same with the other two corners. Now, over the chalk marks write your spirit message, but use a SLATE PENCIL and not CHALK. Cover this writing with the "flap," newspaper side toward the writing.

Have the lights in your seance room slightly lowered. On the table have the newspaper and near it the glass of water, towel and a bit of chalk.

Hand the UNPREPARED SLATE to one of the spectators. In the meantime you clean the prepared slate, going over both the "flap" and unprepared side. With the chalk draw two diagonal lines, on the "flap" similar to those below it, and also on the unprepared side. You can also make on the unprepared side of the prepared slate any distinctive marks that your audience may suggest. This is done to prevent substitution.

The prepared slate is now laid "flap" side down on the newspaper on the table. Go through the same cleaning and marking process with the slate that the spectator holds. When this is accomplished, pick up the prepared slate by the frame, leaving the "flap" behind on the newspaper, where it will not be noticed, owing to its special backing.

Place the two slates together, writing inside of course, and throw your towel carelessly over the flap on the table. Ask one of your audience to hold the slates for a short time, go through some mysterious motions and wierd talk, and upon opening them—to the utter astonishment of all—one of the slates is found to be covered with writing OVER the chalk marks.

Do not attempt presentation of this experiment until you are thoroughly familiar with it. Practise it with the instructions before you, going over each detail carefully until you have mastered them all in your mind. The above is one of the finest experiments in the category of mind reading and telepathy or Spiritualism, if you wish to call it that, when properly presented.

TIED SLATE TESTS USING SUBJECT'S OWN SLATES.

In this experiment we will be brief and to the point; going right into the explanation without devoting time to a lengthy discourse on the "effect" and "method" of presentation.

The subject brings his or her own slates. These are then cleaned and tied together after which they are laid on a stand. The subject then writes the name of the party he wants to hear from on the back of a card or slate given him by the performer. After this is accomplished he holds up the slate or card, blank side to the performer with the writing facing him. The only contact that the performer has with the subject is to hold his hand high and steady. This makes it possible, with the subject in the right position, for a "silent" assistant to look through the back drapes and by use of a pair of field glasses read what is written on the card or slate.

After appearing to concentrate for some minutes and to receive vibrations from the subject's hand, the performer requests him to place the card or small slate in his pocket and to place his hands on the slates that have been washed and tied.

The performer then steps over to the edge of the wing, where a small stand is placed on which is a pitcher of water and a glass. In the act of taking a drink, the performer is told by the "silent" assistant the name of the person from whom the subject wishes to get his message. Returning to the center of the room or stage, the performer seats himself in a chair and proceeds to remain very quiet as though in thought, for several minutes. (In the meantime the slates are lying tied on the table in full view of the audience).

Of a sudden the performer stands up and tells the subject to think of some question that, in his (subject's) mind would do him some good. Placing a chair on either side of the table the performer takes one and beckons the subject to the other. The slates are placed beneath the table, one end being held by the subject and the other by the performer. In the meantime the performer keeps leading the subject on, and without his (the subject's) actually telling what he would like to know, the performer, if he is any student of psychology or human nature at all, will be able to practically guess word for word just what his victim is thinking and would like to know.

As soon as the performer is fairly certain that he is on the right track, he writes plainly his message on the upturned side of the upper slate with a noiseless slate pencil, and at the finish signing the name of the person from which the subject wishes to hear. All this time the performer must talk to the sitter, so that his attention will not become drawn to any unusual activity under the table top. After a few moments jerk the plates from his hands saying:

"I don't think we will get anything. We forgot to put a pencil between the slates."

In the act of bringing the slates to the table top, however, the performer reverses them, so that the writing now faces downward. The string is slipped off and the slates are shown to be still blank (the sides facing each other).

A small slate pencil is placed on the topmost slate, and the one on which the writing is is brought up and placed over it in such a manner that the writing will then be on the inside; the bottom to top movement having been executed without exposing the writing or attracting the attention of the subject and general audience that

PRACTICAL TELEPATHY

anything unusual transpired. The string is rewound about the slates and tied, and once more then are placed beneath the table.

This time, the performer's right hand clasps that of his subject above the table, the slates being held by the left hand of each. The performer runs his finger-nails lightly over the slate surface beneath the table, several time after the scratching stops to "enjoy a few moments is writing. The slates are kept beneath the table for a time after the scartching stops to "enjoy a few moments of intensified" silence, when they are withdrawn and the message is found to be written.

Placing the slates under the table can be dispensed with when they are tied the second time, but it will also necessitate dispensing with the "spirit writing" (scratching). The above must be mastered thoroughly before any performer, either amateur or professional, should attempt to exhibit it in public performance; and in the opinion of the editor, the effect should be avoided as much as possible owing to the many very delicate moves that must be developed down to a perfection. It is, nevertheless, a very beautiful experiment if properly performed, and should be held in reserve for the final of this part of the program.

THE GREAT CHEMICAL SLATE TRICK.

Magicians and Mediumistic pretenders have done a lot of off-hand and yet serious thinking to originate a really practical slate writing trick. Many have come into existence as the result of this, but of the various methods conceived, the following two are the best to my knowledge for all general exhibitions.

CAUSTIC PENCIL.

A single slate should be used in performing this experiment; and the performer should not attempt to perform it with two slates placed together.

Prior to exhibiting your slate-writing powers; write your message on a cheap slate—one of the five cent variety, using a caustic or nitrate of silver pencil. (Be sure that the pencil is of this composition). This can be secured at any drug store at small cost and will last for innumerable performances. The message is written on the slate as you would write with an ordinary pencil.

When the message has been completed, breathe on it, and it will disappear to that degree that the slate can be shown casually as containing no writing, without much danger of the subtefuge being detected.

When you are ready to perform, have your spectator on one side of the table with a soft sponge dipped in a weak solution of salt water, clean the slate thoroughly. When both sides of the slate are wet, it can be freely examined by the sitter without the slightest danger of the writing being detected.

Do not dry the slate but place it (writing down) on four empty thread spools, one under each corner on the table, so that it forms a small stand. (Should you desire, you may have these spools painted or gilded, which will, at least, give a little color to the experiment).

While waiting for the slate to dry, make mysterious passes over it or engage your spectator in conversation. In a few moments turn the slate face up and the message will be found to be written thereon. The writing on the slate, while of acid composition, will very much resemble genuine slate pencil work.

It is not absolutely necessary to employ spools in this experiment, but they are excellent, in that it gives the air a free hand to circulate under and on the prepared side of the slate, therefore causing it to dry quickly. The salt water solution converts the nitrate of silver writing into chloride of silver, and as this latter is a white precipitate, the writing appears in either white or light grey letters. The writing instantly vanishes at the touch of a damp finger, but will reappear as soon as the slate dries. You can, however, use a slate only once for this experiment—hence the reason for using those of cheap quality.

In presenting this effect, you can say to your spectator or spectators:

"Let's see what luck we have in securing automatic or spiritualistic writing."

You then write a message with an ordinary slate pencil, read it aloud and then wipe it off with your hand. Tell them you will write another, but this time use the caustic pencil. Read that and then wash off the slate with the sponge and salt solution. What you really do is to write the message that you will eventually show your audience (with caustic pencil) and in pretending to read it to them, make up something wholly different.

ANOTHER CHEMICAL SLATE.

Take some ordinary library paste and make a very weak dilution of it with water. With a small brush cover one side of the slate completely with this solution. While the slate is still wet write in your message with an ordinary slate pencil. The paste solution will "fix" it to the slate. When exhibiting the slates wash them with a sponge dipped in alcohol, and they can then be freely shown (while wet) in the ordinary dim light of the seance room, the alcohol darkening the writing and rendering it invisible. Dry the slates lightly with a piece of soft cloth, tie them together—prepared sides facing each other—and when opened the message will appear. Should the slates be washed in water, the message would at once rub off. To avoid the presence of the alcohol being detected, incense should be burned if possible.

This method is more suitable for large halls and the stage than for small gatherings. It has been very successfully used by Dr. Herron in his notable Hall Seances.

CHAPTER SEVEN

PRACTICAL TELEPATHY

CHAPTER SEVEN

DOLPH JAGGERS, VERSATILE MAGICIAN AND SPECIALTY ARTIST—BRIEF BIOGRAPHICAL SKETCH—CONFESSIONS OF A MYSTERY MAN.

Dolph Jaggers was born April 27th, 1890, near Marysville, Ohio. He was in his ninth year when he first witnessed the performance of a magician. W. W. Durbin of Kenton, Ohio, was the "professor."

It was at the age of fourteen that Dolph started his career as a showman, having signed contracts with the "Adam Fitzer's Big One-Ring Overhead Shows," to do a batton juggling act. The following season found him "ballyhoooing" in front of a carnival show. During that season the mystery bug got in its work on the lad and he began mystifying the "natives" by having them tie him to a chair; after which he would make his escape in full view without untying the knots.

Since that time he has been connected with various shows, such as carnivals, vaudeville, medicine, benefits and circuses. This artist always has an excellent repertoire of escapes at his command.

Few performers, indeed, could boast of such a wide range of accomplishments and skill as can this specialty artist. As an escapist, he has few equals. Other specialties of his consist in light and heavy-weight balancing, ventriloquism, and juggling. He is also a clever magician, comedian and mind-reader.

His magical performances date back only a half dozen years or so, but he is one of the few public performers who are original in practically everything they do or say. He has made improvements on several old tricks, but the majority of his offerings are of his own invention and construction. He has about a dozen big stage illusions. While a few of these are, as yet, incomplete, the most of them he has brought to a state of perfection, and represent the full bloom of development of his own oriignal ideas and conceptions. Original ideas are, and always have been, his motto.

Three times now he has tried vaudeville road shows of his own, but without any marked success. Despite these reserves, though he has come up smiling each time, after having learned an expensive lesson. Once lately, assisted by his beautiful and charming young wife, he has gone into the mystery game (mind reading and cabinet work) and it appears that he is, at last, on the road to success in his chosen field.

CONFESSIONS.

During my years of facing the public, as an escapist and exponent of the allied arts, I have acquired a world of knowledge, some of which, dear reader, I shall attempt to impart to you. Contrary to the opinions of some, that it is inadvisable, I always work my cabinet escapes first, as the audience so far, are resting under the impression that you have nothing to offer them that they cannot see into. But at the proper time you turn the tables, and work your "outside" stuff, such as ropes, chains, torture board, pillory, straight jackets, etc., which always gives your performance a finished and polished final, amid the applause which you are bound to receive if the act is properly worked up; a point that remains solely up to each individual. I will now give you some tips which I hope may prove of some value to you.

All of my stuff is "lobby-proof," even though left in the lobby of the theatre for the purpose of examination. My mail bag is different from the majority I have ever seen, as I use *no* steel bar. The bag measures 36 inches in width and 72 inches in length, with double seam down each side. Hem at top is 3 inches wide which is also double seamed. Around the top are seven iron loops about 2 inches long and ¾ inch wide. These are placed about 4 inches apart. They must be sewn solidly to canvas (preferably by a harness maker). Next, a length of leather strap, with a staple riveted on one end is shown, also an R. F. D. mail-box lock with keyhole in bottom; this is essential. Strap is now threaded through loops and pulled taut, so that you may know just where to put slot in strap to fit your staple. After being locked in, you make your escape in the following manner:

You will find enough room left in mouth of sack through which to push a duplicate key, which you have concealed on your person. Grasp key with other hand by getting slack enough in bag. Now the key is on the outside of bag, and you are on the inside; still your fingers tightly clasp two thicknesses of canvas with key in between. Grasp lock the same way as you have the key; and as the keyhole is hanging down, with a little feeling around you can insert the key. Remove lock and strap from staple, pull bag free from strap, get out, thread strap back thru loops, replace lock, conceal duplicate key and make appearance.

I usually attach thread to key and to my belt so that should I drop key during any of my maneuvering I still have not lost it. The lock key-hole can be sealed by means of adhesive tape, procurable at druggists. The committee can write their own initials on tape and place it on lock. All you have to do is to roll tape back from keyhole to insert key. After having made your delivery roll tape back over keyholoe.

I have found that the best way to learn handcuffs is to buy all the different makes—second hand if possible— tear them apart, examine the locks and see what shape pick will work the lock. Experience has taught me that a hair pin is a handy article to have about during an escape act. This can be wound around the ring finger, and concealed by a large set or wedding ring of wide pattern. A common button hook straightened out makes a good pick for several different cuffs. This can be concealed in trousers waist-band, one in front and one behind. With a little practice, you can escape from the figure eight cuffs no matter how they are placed upon you. Always keep a thread on all picks and keys as sometimes you are liable to drop something and the "talking" it does is always a knock for your act. I might add that a short length of corset steel often proves helpful.

The idea of smuggling an automobile jack into a common packing box with which to pry off a board must be a joke. A much simpler and less expensive outfit which can easily be concealed about the person, consists of one round-headed bolt 3 inches lang by $\frac{1}{4}$ inch in diameter; one large screw eye; one nut for bolt, and a straightened shoe buttoner. Just below the head of bolt, the latter is square. Into each of these four sides have a hole drilled into which you can insert your straightened button hook which you use as a lever with which you turn the bolt.

After you are nailed up in the box (which is usually made of pine), you screw the screw-eye into end of box about one and one-half inches down from the lid opposite the center of board which you wish to pry off. Screw nut onto bolt so that the latter will project thru the nut. Insert screw-end of bolt thru screw-eye allowing nut to rest on screw-eye. Now, by turning the bolt the head of the latter will press against the board which you wish to pry loose. The use of your buttoner inserted in the drilled holes of the bolt, will do the trick for you. In making your escape, don't forget to take with you the little implements which have served you so well. In hammering home the nails in the board again, use your rubber-heeled shoe.

If nails used in making the box are of a blunt nature, they will be much more easily removed. I have often found that a little humping of my back was all that was necessary to pry boards off. A flash light is often a very useful accessory in box escapes, especially for the novice; but I seldom ever use one for this purpose.

A very good trunk escape—done anywhere—can easily be prepared without a bit of outlay. Get a trunk that has a lock made as follows: A sort of a button enters slot made for it. Key turns lock or button and trunk is locked. Now unlock trunk and drill hole thru wood beneath where lock comes so that you can turn the button of lock from inside with your two straightened button hooks. Drill a small hole in lid thru wood and metal where snap fasteners come at each end, and use buttonhooks to push snaps or staples out until they are free from fasteners. If trunk has straps on it—cut straps off before performing. Use a flash-light if necessary—it quickens your escape sometimes.

For barrel escape, I have three hinge hasps on solid lid. Three extra long staples riveted to a square piece of iron are shoved thru three slots in barrel corresponding to hasps on lid. These are all locked with performer inside up to his neck in water. Keyholes on locks are sealed.

Explanation: You have duplicate keys. The above staples are shown, but only one of them is really used. You have concealed two duplicates which are not rivited, but have nuts in each shank. You, of course, remove nuts, push staples thru slots, raise up lid, get out, unlock the two locks, place real (good) staples in slots in barrel, lock lid on as it was originally; conceal fake staples, replace seals on locks and make appearance. I use the same system of sealing in all my lock escapes. Adhesive tape is procurable at any druggist.

My pillory is made of two pieces of 2 x 6 inch timber, 30 inches long. Holes are cut out to fit around the wrists and neck. A hinge is at one end and staple and hasp are at the other. I am locked in and the keyhole sealed. A cloth is thrown over me and in less than one minute I remove cloth—a free man—with pillory still locked; and keyhole still sealed.

Explanation: I file right wrist hole slightly larger than left one and grease it; also the other two holes. Now with a little work, I can extricate my right hand, obtain concealed key; unlock pillory; remove from neck and other wrist; relock everything; replace tapes and throw off the cloth; and pillory, lock, etc., can be examined.

Now, kind reader, study over the above and see where you can make improvements. I must admit I don't know it all; but there is always a chance of one knowing something which is not known by the other fellow. Only by the exchange of ideas and our experiences and thru mutual helpfulness can our art, as such, enfold and expand and evolve the beauty and degree of perfection which I am sure, we all long so much that our art shall attain.

ILLUSIONS.

I very much doubt that there ever was an aspirant to magic who did not at sometime long for a levitation equipment. But to many of us, the prohibitive cast frustrated our ambitions. I was one of those lads myself. But I got busy, used my head and finally made one, or rather several different patterns. If you already have an "Aga" and would like to devise some means of using it at clubs, churches, schoolhouses, and other places where assistant can't get under stage; here is where I will make an effort to come to your rescue.

Get a bar of steel about six feet long—same size as suspension bar. Bore two $\frac{1}{2}$ inch holes about 6 or 8 inches apart in one end of same. Now do the same in goose neck or suspension bar where it comes around back of the body—making three holes to correspond with holes in steel. Bend steel to fit curve (back of body). Make a slot in curtain (perpendicular), about 18 inches long. Steel is pushed thru slot. Now in this end of steel a $\frac{7}{8}$ inch hole is bored. A length of $2\frac{1}{2}$ inch gas pipe with flange at one end is to be solidly screwed to the floor, has a hole bored in top and corresponding to hole in steel, so that when steel is bolted to pipe, it will move up and down but has little side play.

To raise lady in air, an automobile jack is placed on a solid block. The top of the pack is fastened to underside of steel just back of curtain. A small black wood block is nailed to the floor to keep jack from slipping. When we give the assistant the tip he pumps jack which raises steel which, in turn, is attached to gooseneck or suspension bar, and behold The lady *leviates*. After the usual hoop passing, the lady is lowered to a somewhat safer, if not so interesting position.

Points of advantage in this arrangement are:

You can, apparently, walk around the "sleeping beauty." You don't have to stand in one position while the levitation takes place; the cost is nominal. I made my apparatus complete, exclusive of black drop, at an actual outlay of only $10.00.

Should you have occasion to use this on the ground, drive stakes and fasten a small platform to them and on this bolt your pipe flange. You will find this outfit packs well, and does not weigh any more than the old style of apparatus.

BEAUTIFUL SUBSTITUTION.

The lower half of central panel is removed from folding screen, and folded to form an enclosure. Lady garbed in flowing gown open all way down in front, enters enclosure from rear. She poses with back to open panel, enabling audience to see lower part of gown or robe. Performer fires shot, removes screen and the robe reveals his male assistant! Lady having vanished.

Explanation: Work over a trap or near exit. When lady enters, she removes robe, suspending same to hooks so that it will cover open space in panel; make her exit, male assistant enters, dons robe, and gives performer the cue.

EGYPTIAN MUMMY.

A box about 4 feet long, 18 inches wide, and 12 inches deep, is shown; bottom removed, showing and proving box to be unmistakably empty. Bottom is replaced and box lifted on backs of two chairs, and lid put on. Shot is fired, lid removed, and the box stood on end, revealing an Egytian mummy.

Explanation: The mummy is fastened with a piece of fine black silk thread to the back of the lid. As all attention and splurge is centered on the displaying of the box, the fact that the lid was not shown on both sides escapes the attention of the audience. In placing the lid on the box always place front side first; this gives you a chance to sever the thread, allowing the mummy shell (it being made of paper mache) to fall into the box, after which the lid and box can be shown on all sides.

CHAPTER EIGHT

PRACTICAL TELEPATHY

CHAPTER EIGHT
SUPPLEMENT AND GLOSSARY.
TELEPATHIC TEST.

The following can be used excellently with the blood writing or pellet test. Ask one of your spectators (we assume he is endowed with ordinary intelligence) to select a number, mentally, between "one" and "ten," and to fix his mind firmly on that number. Take hold of the spectator's or subject's hand and looking fixedly into his eyes, say: "You are thinking of number seven." Nine persons out of ten will choose seven. It is, of course, obvious that this experiment should not be worked more than once.

In case you fail it will not be to your discredit, especially if you have been mystifying a group of people continually for any length of time. Any audience will allow for one failure.

To simplify the experiment and practically cinch it for yourself, before telling the spectator what number he is thinking of ask him if it is "odd" or "even." Odd will be "seven," while even is invariably "six."

SPIRIT MESSAGES ON ARM.

Write a message upon the inside of your right forearm with real blood (if available) or red ink. This is, of course, done before-hand. In showing your bared arm to the audience; sans any messages; roll up the sleeve and raise the arm in such a manner so that you will be looking into your right palm. (In this manner the inside forearm cannot be seen). In dropping the arm, turn it quickly so that the inside forearm will be facing your body. The general impression is that you have shown both sides of your arm.

PRACTICAL TELEPATHY

HALEY'S SPIRIT MESSAGE ON ARM.

The message should be written on the arm with liquid potassa, using a clean pen. To the center of a dark handkerchief attach a small sponge dipped in tincture of tumeric. After burning the slip on which the spectator has written his or her question, and casting the ashes over the arm, rub the arm with the prepared sponge, concealed by the handkerchief, and the writing will come out on the flesh in blood-red letters. Inasmuch as the tumeric, when applied, renders the flesh a slightly yellowish color, it is advisable to perform this experiment only under artificial light.

IMPROVED SPIRIT SEANCE.

The reader is undoubtedly familiar with many of the experiments in which "lazy tongs" and fake fingers are employed. I have done away with the latter making it possible, with my method, to move my fingers at any time.

The right hand top corner of the handkerchief contains a hook which is concealed by the fingers. The opposite corner is held by the fingers of the left hand. In making a double cross of his arms to display both sides of the fabric, the performer hooks the pin into his coat. In this manner, the performer can use his right hand freely to ring bells, write on slates etc., or else obtain a load from his body or the table. Although the handkerchief is apparently held suspended between both hands, a large load can be obtained from the body and deliberately placed upon an undraped table. It is needless to say that there are unlimited ways in which this wrinkle can be employed to advantage.

SPIRIT WATCH.

Secure a watch of the hunting-case variety. Remove the crystal and bend the minute hand (the longer of the two) down a little so that when the hands are turned around, it will "trip" a little on the hour hand. When the watch is closed and you are turning the hands around, you can feel the minute hand "tick" as it passes over the hour hand.

In presenting this experiment have the watch set at about quarter to twelve. Give it to a spectator for examination, showing him that the hand moves freely by simply turning the stem. Then close the case, and give the watch stem three or four turns, keeping track of each "tick" that you feel. You will have no difficulty at any time during the winding process—if you keep track of the "ticks"—in telling just what hour the hands point to. This can be worked excellently in connection with the spirit slates.

MEDIUM'S TABLET.

Procure a tablet of moderately thin paper. Coat the underside of the third sheet by lightly rubbing it with a preparation of cold wax. This is prepared by melting some paraffin over a water bath and adding a little vaseline—just enough to color it slightly yellow—and allowing it to cool.

Run through the tablet quickly, thereby showing your spectators that there is nothing to it but blank sheets. The top one is torn off, on the pretense that it is soiled, and the tablet handed to one of the spectators with the request that he write a message thereon, or anything that his fancy may dictate. He is then requested to tear off this sheet and put it in his pocket. To read the waxed impression of the message, it is necessary to dust upon the prepared sheet some lamp black, which is then lightly rubbed into the paper with a soft cloth. This brings out the message clearly. It can readily be seen that unless you have an assistant, this is hardly an extemporaneous experiment, but is excellent for the occasion wherein you you will give the spectator his message or answer—whatever the case may be—at a later date, or over the phone.

PRACTICAL TELEPATHY

UNPREPARED PADS FOR MESSAGE READING.

I have used both the old carbon and the waxed pads but the people are wise to them, not the common people, but generally those kind who have read books upon this subject, and I know from experience that this class are worse than the ignorant person. They go to the theatre with the sole intention of queering the performer; to let their friends and others know how smart they art. I have seen this class deliberately cap out a pad on me, put it under their coat and take it home with them, just to find out things.

I never cared so much for this part of it, but some of these wisenheimers would tell the audience near them how it was done. (I have also seen magicians do this, trying to queer a real performer). Why they do this, I do not know unless it is natural of the heart.

Nowadays I seldom use the pad system, but sometimes the performer is compelled to use them. I have experimented for a long time on how to get results with an unprepared pad. It came to me from watching my little girl write her lesson with a hard pencil on a common, ordinary penny pad. I noticed she had to press hard with a hard pencil to do her writing, which left an impression on the lower sheet.

I experimented in developing this impression with Plumbago (lead dust). Also tried gold and silver bronze; the latter two are cleaner. I tried it out on the public and I have used it ever since with good results. Even for office work, it even fools the wisenheimers; it saves labor in preparing special pads; they are always ready.

Madame Helms, Madame Emerson, the Jewess and others to whom I sold this are using them with good success. I can recommend this for picture theatre work especially, where four or five shows are given nightly. I have also used prepared pads rubbed over with cocoa butter or common soap, because I had nothing else handy when I was in a hurry, and I got results. However, I

PRACTICAL TELEPATHY

have done away with all of this since adopting the plain penny pads and hard pencils.

In 5 and 10 cent theatres where from 3 to 5 shows are given, no spirit cabinet act is necessary (a la Anna Eva Fay). To get possession of the pads in order to develop the questions and put suitable replies to them behind stage or dressing room, the pads are passed out before each show, when orchestra is playing (ushers can help you do this), and people are requested to write their questions. Use your own hard pencils; from 10 to 15 questions are plenty in 5 and 10 cent theatres, for each show.

As some of these picture theatres have no dressing rooms or stages, you have to use a curtain and arrange a developing room. When show starts the professor takes the pads from the people and the ushers take them into the developing room and bring out the writing with gold dust which is rubbed over sheet of paper with velvet. This brings out the writing (the impression caused by hard pencil).

Lady copies the message also the names—looks over the list of stock answers and puts suitable answer to each question.

In an opera house with large audiences, I never develop or read all the questions. I use from 25 to 35 pads in big theatres. I figure 10 to 12 minutes for each show in a picture treatre, 20 minutes for handbills and 30 to 40 minutes with my own show in opera house. If longer, it gets tiresome. It is not necessary to read all the messages, especially when the performer intends to spring "stock messages" or 1, 2 or 3 boosters. (Altho this act can be done without boosters), which makes it stronger and predictions can also be made at the conclusion of the act.

PRACTICAL TELEPATHY

(Being Suggestions for Handbills or other Advertising, etc.)

(HANDBILL WITH CUT)

(Name of Theatre)

Date_____

A Strange Man With a Strange Power

MAR-JAH

The Wise Man of India
Ask him anything

Love, Business,
Marriage, Investment

Psychic Marvel

What will 1924 be? Are you going to Travel? The Wonderful Yogi from the Far East.

Special Announcement!

Marjah will give a special matinee for women only, Wednesday Afternoon, Jan. 14th, at 2:30.

If you are married or in trouble, come and consult him. Also Private Reading

FREE!

To the first 100 women who enter theatre at this matinee.

MONDAY
Commencing Jan 3, 1922
A Strange Man With a Strange Power
ENGAGEMENT EXTRAORDINARY
(In addition to Photoplay Program)
Ask Him Anything
PSYCHIC MARVEL
What Will 1924 Be?

Love
Business
Marriage
Investment
Is Your Wife
Huband
Sweetheart
True?

SEE   HEAR   ASK!

Marjah of India, master mind reader and crystal gazer — the Wonderful Man of Mystery! To him the past is like an open book—the future like a crystal.
He will answer all questions! He will advise you truthfully and fully!

Knows All!
Sees All!   Tells All!

THE ABSOLUTE MASTER!
THE WONDER WORKER!

Prof   (Your name here)

Presenting a different performance nightly in High Class Magic, etc., etc., and a Baffling Demonstration in

MIND READING   CRYSTAL GAZING
and VOODOOISM!

The First Time in This City. A Study of Human Nature, Psychology, in which he reads your Innermost Thoughts. He Pierces the Mystery of the Soul and which has prompted thousands to say:

HOW DOES HE DO IT?

No Matter What You Want to Know—Ask Him, He Knows!

A few of the many questions you may wish to ask:

When and where will I marry? When will I get my divorce? Is it advisable to have an operation? Is my husband true? Will I win my lawsuit? Should I sell my property? Should I hold my stocks and bonds? Will I inherit a fortune? Who stole my automobile? Where is my sweetheart (or relatives)? Whether it concerns business investments, lawsuits, domestic or social affairs, separations, divorces or engagements, etc., etc.

ASK HIM!

Hand bills such as suggested in accompanying specimens will be found good advertising for opening night when sealed questions effects—such as "CRUSHING BAFFLER" as explained on page 5, are to be demonstrated. These specimen hand bills are merely to assist the aspirant in getting up his advertising matter which can, of course, be arranged in accordance with his own idea. Newspapers can generally be used to good advantage also. An account of this character requires stirring publicity.

PRACTICAL TELEPATHY

Use this form to write questions on, and be sure you seal envelope tight. Bring it to theatre, sign your name in full or your initials. Write your questions at home—seal in your own envelope.

Name or Initials_____

Street and No._____

Question _____

In many towns fortune telling is not allowed. I have formed a card so as to forestall any kick.

THIS COUPON ENTITLES THE BEARER TO A PERSONAL INTERVIEW WITH
PROF _____
With the distinct understanding that he is not a fortune teller and that you are seeking his advice only.
Name _____
Address _____
Time of Appointment_____

WORTHWHILE REMINDERS

PRACTICAL TELEPATHY

NOW IN PREPARATION

"NEW ERA MAGIC"

By Joseph Ovette.

Joseph Ovette needs no introduction as a capable writer of magical literature. His six previous works, "MAGICIAN'S NEW FIELD," "TRICKERY TRICKS," "ADVANCED MAGIC," "GRANDDADDY'S OLD ARM CHAIR" or "THE TRIPLE MYSTERY," a manuscript, "VAUDEVILLE MAGIC" and "BARGAIN MAGIC," enjoyed a tremendous sale, in several instances running into three and four editions and brought the author fame.

Now comes "NEW ERA MAGIC," which is destined to become one of the classics of magical literature. Not only is it by far the most elaborate, comprehensive and valuable book that Mr. Ovette has written to date, but it is one of the choicest pieces of magical literature that has EVER been written by ANYONE.

Among some the features will be a chapter devoted to the latest MIRACLES in card manipulation, which will include all of Mr. Ovette's famous four-ace tricks and a host of new ones; a chapter embracing handkerchief manipulation par excellence; a chapter on intricite and astonishing thimble manipulation, in addition to chapters on all other phases of conjuring.

One whole section of this remarkable book will be devoted to the latest illusion creations.

Now under the process of revision by Preston Langley Hickey.

Watch For It!   Wait For It!   Inquire About It!

For further information address inquiries to:

JOSEPH OVETTE,
44 Flushing Ave., Brooklyn, N. Y.

PRACTICAL TELEPATHY

GRANDDADDY'S OLD ARM CHAIR
OR
THE TRIPLE MYSTERY

EFFECTS

A hand truck loaded with what looks to be pieces of furniture, and which is in reality parts of one article of furniture, namely: An Upholstered Chair, is wheeled on the stage. The load consists of five pieces or parts which, when assembled, forms a large easy arm chair, complete.

Now, as the performer and his assistant unloads the truck, they assemble the five parts, forming the chair complete, in full view of the audience. The following is the mode of procedure in detail:

First, the legs are placed on the stage. Next the cushion seat is shown, also, the reverse side of which is turned to the audience that they may see the underside contains only springs and springs only. Performer thrusts his wand among the springs to prove only empty space there. The cushion is then placed, forming the seat.

NEXT, the back is adjusted—then the arms are put in place. The chair, which is on casters, is now whirled around, so that the audience can get a good view of rear side of chair.

(The chair-back is made with a door that opens, giving full view of interior of chair-back). Performer states that his Father was very wealthy and when he died he willed him his "Old Arm-Chair." This gave occasion for my relatives and others to snicker and laugh and poke fun at me because my grandfather left me nothing but "The Old Arm-Chair!"

"But, shortly I turned the laugh on them," says the performer, "when one day I discovered a secret—I discovered that the chair had a dor opening into its interior!"

Suiting action to his words, the performer opens the door of the Chair-back; thus giving audience full view of interioor of Chair-back, which contains springs and springs only. Performer pokes his wand all among the springs which proves the statement true. Performer further states that it was in the secret enclosure that he found Eight hundred thousand dollars ($800,000) in gold and legal tender! But, says the performer, the closet is—is—empty—now!

The door of the Chair-back is now closed and the chair is turned half way around again leaving chair facing audience.

Next, an ordinary looking wooden box—soap box—is shown on all sides and placed on the Chair Seat where front side, hinged as a door is opened giving full view of interior of the box. Performer taps with his wand all around on inside of box to show all to be just as it looks—Perfectly Empty!

MYSTERY NO. 1.

Performer closes door of box—Crack! Crack! The report of pistol shot rings out and instantly a huge bowl 30 inches in diameter appears upon the box. (Note:—Box measures 20 inches across either way, while the bowl is 30 inches in diameter!)

NOTE these points: There are no mirrors used. No stage traps. There is no other furniture on the stage. The materialization takes place in full view and without any covering, and in the center of a brilliantly lighted stage. No "Black Art" Wings, Drops, Screens, etc. etc., have nothing to do with this scheme. The view underneath the Chair remains perfectly clear all the time. Unadulterated "New Era Magic." Baffles the most astute and analetycal intellects. Most wonderful magic the world has ever known!

MYSTERY NO. 2.

No sooner than the huge bowl appears, a stream of "Blood" spurts from center of bowl several feet up into the air where it makes a graceful curve and falls back into the bowl which soon becomes full to overflowing.

NOTE THE POINTS—No connection with water works or slaughterhouse. Performer does not go near the bowl.

MYSTERY NO. 3.

Thunders roar—terrible detonation and confusion, (like a third act in melo-drama) and suddenly on the surface of the blood in the bowl appears a bewilderingly strange and most wonderful sight—a sight fairly staggering in its amazing effect!

An Allegorical Wonder which, thruout the ages, has only existed in the imagination but which now appears real and alive! Yes, very much alive! This strangest of all freaks is known as a Mermaid—A FISH WITH A HUMAN HEAD!!! A HUMAN HEAD OF THE FEMALE SPECIES!!!

While the audience is watching the play of the "fountain of blood" a tail of a monster fish is suddenly seen to appear flapping about in the bowl! This would seem the limit—but what stage of consternation do you suppose the mental faculties of the audience is thrown into when the head of the fish appears and rests its chin over the rim of the bowl?

After an interesting and amusing conversation between the performer and the "Mermaid" wherein comedy plays the leading part act closes with a song by the MERMAID accompanied by the orchestra.

Dear Professor: Do you aspire to fame and a mcopetence? _Well, you can easily achieve both. Get the above illusion and stage it— that's all!

You have been calling yourself "Great" for some time, now haven't you, professor? Very well, now why not change things around and let your audience daub you "Great," they will do it, if you take our advice. The above illusion

GRANDDADDY'S OLD ARM CHAIR
OR
THE TRIPLE MYSTERY

is an illusion of the Higher order. The New Era Quality and makes a vaudeville act complete. Will book you across the continent and back as a Head-Liner, with as many return dates as you want, and within a year you will be getting offers from Great Britain and other European Countries. So you will have no more time to hang around Booking Offices waiting for some vaudeville artist to get sick and the tune that "magic is dead," will sound to you like a comic song. Manuscript with patter and blue print sketches will be furnished for $3.00. (ARE YOU WISE?)

JOSEPH OVETTE
44 Flushing Ave., Brooklyn, N. Y.

PRACTICAL TELEPATHY

KING TUT'S PILL BOX

EFFECT

A spectator writes his name on a slip of paper. He is now given a small paper box, into which he is asked to place the slip containing his name. This done, he is given another box, slightly larger than the first, into which he places the latter and covers. This is followed out once more, making a nest of three boxes in all. (Bear in mind that this entire procedure is done by the spectator and not the performer.)

When everyone is satisfied that things so far are on the square, the performer removes a small black box from his pocket, with two smaller boxes within it, making another nest, and in the third box is found the slip of paper containing the spectator's name.

This is an exceptionally valuable little piece of apparatus for mind reading acts. There are no confederates, palming, changing or transfer of writing.

With every order for King Tut's Pill Box, I include free the VISUAL VISION CRYSTAL GAZING ACT, the latest and most practical method for any performer.

Price Complete, $3.00

JOSEPH OVETTE

44 Flushing Avenue   Brooklyn, N. Y.

SPIRITUALISTIC
AND
MIND READING MYSTERIES

The time is now here for Modernism.

If you wish success, you must use successful methods.

Strike out and thread down your individual road to fame.

Forget the fancies of yesterday, come down to earth and start with fresh ideas of merit.

Ideas Are My Specialty!
Showmanship Is My Food!

Let me help you as I have already helped a number of big ones.

I have some of the finest and highest class methods of procedure and presentation.

If it is anything in the line of Magic or Spiritualism, consult me first.

JOSEPH OVETTE

44 Flushing Avenue   Brooklyn, N. Y.

CPSIA information can be obtained at www.ICGtesting.com
Printed in the USA
LVOW02s2245030414

380170LV00003B/62/A